CUSTOMER EXPERIENCE3

28 international CX professionals share their current best-thinking on achieving impact and visibility through worldclass best-practice CX

W&M

Customer Experience 3

Edited by Naeem Arif, Andrew Priestley

First published in March 2021

www.writingmatterspublishing.com

ISBN 978-1-912774-81-4 (Pbk)

ISBN 978-1-912774-80-7 (eBk)

A CIP catalogue record for this book is available from the British Library.

Contents

Foreword: CX At The Crossroads Of New Possibilities

Neil Skehel

Over the years, I've had the privilege of seeing customer experience evolve into a global movement that's changing organisations everywhere for the better. What a journey it's been! When we founded the UK Customer Experience Awards back in 2010, the Customer Experience Professional's Association was still a twinkle in someone's eye. Even then, I knew it was a movement with incredible potential and I've always been proud to recognise extraordinary achievements in this field.

This book is a reflection of how much the discipline has evolved in the past decade, and its chapters are a sign of the intellectual maturity, creativity and emotional intelligence of CX thought leaders around the world. The contributors hail from many different countries, cultures and backgrounds, but they're united by a common commitment: to enhance our appreciation of the many aspects of customer experience, and to deepen commitment to it in our own organisations. There's a welcome mix of quantitative and qualitative analysis in here, with plenty of real-world case studies to accompany theoretical approaches. This is the kind of understanding we need to take the CX discipline to the next stage in its evolution.

You see, in 2021, CX is at a crossroads of possibilities.

The last decade has seen pioneers take on the challenge, at times a lonely one, of putting customer experience on the lips of company directors around the globe. There's been substantial success in that area, and a huge number of organisations are now speaking the language of customer experience – a huge achievement in itself.

The next decade, and the aftermath of the global pandemic, will determine whether we can embed CX as a priority for shareholders and fully convince them of the business imperative of putting customers at the heart of what they do. The ideas and strategies featured in this book give me great confidence that this can, and will, be achieved. After all, it's only by showing the tangible commercial benefits of a CX-driven approach – speaking in language that shareholders understand – that large organisations will get the fullest possible commitment to their CX vision. And this book contains enormous evidence of that!

CX3 showcases an extraordinary community of CX thinkers, one that's growing all the time. As the CXPA's Global Partner in Advancing CX, Awards International is always keen to shine a light on best practice in the CX space, and you'll find no shortage of that in this remarkable book. There are new ideas for you to pick up, problems for you to ponder, and solutions for you to enact!

I hope you enjoy your read, and that you gain the recognition you deserve for taking the next steps on your journey.

With best wishes,

Neil Skehel

CEO, Awards International

Welcome To Customer Experience 3

Welcome to our third book in our *Customer Experience* series. One again, we aim to showcase best practice, concepts and case studies from high performing practitioners and consultants from around the world.

Customer Experience is not a new concept. I would argue that it has been the secret sauce to most successful businesses throughout history. I often quote the example of a 'General Store' maybe 100 years ago, that served a local community; the owner would know you personally and source products that they knew their clientele wanted.

Fast forward through the decades and is it much different?

Customers still want a personal service and they still want to be appreciated. The big difference now is that they have infinitely more options and are swamped for choice of where to spend their money. Businesses that deliberately offer a remarkable customer centric experience tend to out-perform businesses where the experience is a random, happy accident; or worse non-existent.

Some of the best examples of Customer Centric behaviour can be seen in some of the smallest organisations. Common sense tells them that if they can create happy customers, then they will always be in business. And herein lies the simplest fact for any business professional, irrespective of their industry or sector;

"Customer Experience, is not an initiative, it is a common sense business strategy that applies to every organisation."

Whilst everyone will remember the negative impact of the global pandemic, I would like to highlight the positive business impacts that we have seen. We have had no choice but to provide our Customers with an aligned in-person and on-line customer experience through digital channels. It was necessary, for both customers and businesses to overcome both their fears and their preferences in order to deal with the 'new normal'.

The experts in CX3 simply urge you to make your customer experiences positive, remarkable and deliberate.

A Gartner research paper in 2014 made a prediction about 2020 that has strangely become a prophecy fulfilled.

89% of companies expect to compete mostly on Customer Experience by 2020

Gartner 2014 Study of Marketeer's

Customer experience thought leader, Shaun Smith said, *"Your customer cannot NOT have an experience. The question is: was the experience the one you really intended?"*

If your customer is having an experience ... *anyway*, it may as well be one you are in control of. One that is customer-centric, deliberate, designed, intentional, consistent, memorable and valued. And one that makes sense to the customer.

In one way or another, every article in CX3 supports this basic philosophy.

PS: If you are reading this book and have an article you'd love to share, we want to hear about it for our upcoming projects. In the first instance, you can reach out to me and I will try and connect your story to an audience.

About Naeem Arif

Naeem has three decades of experience as a retail business owner and CX consultant with specific expertise in the customer retention functions. During his time he has had the opportunity to work with senior leaders and is known for 'putting the customer first' into every solution he designs.

As well as writing several books, he is the founder of the Customer Experience book series and can be contacted through the following social channels.

Contacts And Links

Naeem@NAConsulting.co.uk

Twitter @NAConsultingLtd

LinkedIn @NaeemArif

Facebook @NAConsultingLtd

1. Customer Centric Culture

The right mindset, attitude and commitment

Understanding Behavioural Economics To Improve The Customer Experience; Identifying Patterns In Consumer Decision Making, Judgements And Behaviour

Richard Jordan

For CX professionals, understanding that a consumer's unconscious beliefs will have an impact upon the products they buy has become an exciting proposition for anyone who hopes to improve the customer experience. After all, if we can understand what a customer believes we can help shape our products and services to improve sales!

Users of Facebook, Amazon and eBay likely understand that when they buy a product or engage in a service they contribute to the production and analysis of data and it is through this process where data-driven marketing strategies are created. But aren't we forgetting something? How do we know what brought the customer to want the product in the first place? Why do we buy products from one brand and not another? Why are we influenced by marketing and why do we return to the businesses we trust?

It is within this space that Behavioural Economists analyse the consumer, their behaviours, emotions, thoughts and feelings, as it is in *this* data where successive behaviours are predicted and successful marketing strategies begin.

So, what are the factors which influence a customer's decision making and how can we, as CX professionals use this understanding to improve the customer experience?

In this chapter we will investigate how our emotions, behaviours, thoughts, feelings and memories affect our decision making, how consumerism and popular culture has been shaped by intuitive and irrational decision making and how unconscious biases can actually help the Behavioural Economist.

We might consider the CX professional a relatively new prospect, but as early as the 19th century pioneering thinkers were already investigating the foundations of unconscious beliefs and their impact on social economics. In fact, most contemporary Neuromarketing and Consumer Psychology strategies use models created over 100 years ago by behavioural Psychologists such as John B. Watson (1878–1958) and Edward Lee Thorndike (1874–1949). Their early studies into behaviour found that decisions are influenced by the conditionable and predictable output of learned responses and that it was through the study of a person's interaction with their environment where accurate predictions (and manipulations) of successive behaviours could be created.

At a time when proponents of the emerging Natural Sciences were facing increasing criticism from established scientific and religious communities, Watson and Thorndike's radical view that a consumers free-will was in fact perhaps 'determinable' came as a difficult and questionable observation, but as it turns out one which was both psychologically and commercially valuable. It was through their studies of predictable, rational and emotive behaviours where the psychological community found its greatest insight into consumer behaviour and where the CX community was borne.

Following Watson and Thorndike's early theories, research studies conducted throughout the 1950s (Dahl et al. 1959) found that many business schools were creating strategies for commercial markets and had begun to develop their theoretical and academic research programs to support these lucrative investors.

As consumer/ behaviourist interest developed into psychological economics, an understanding of consumer's thoughts, desires and experiences developed which the commercial and financial markets received with open arms. After all, if businesses could identify *which* products and services a consumer would purchase and *why*, then wasn't it likely that *more* products and services could be sold?

As studies into the psychology of consumer behaviour helped commercial entities to understand how influential marketing, product placement and service availability can be it is interesting to note this affection was only surpassed by the consumers themselves. Where consumerism before the application of research into psychological influence was successful, tailoring marketing strategies to target specific consumer demographics saw unprecedented success for businesses that began to use Neuromarketing strategies. One only has to consider the gender-specific advertisements of tobacco and domestic goods in the 1950's to see how marketing for a specific social group improved sales and how creating a link between products and social status triggered intrinsic and unconscious beliefs in the consumer.

It was within this exciting mid-century period of emerging Behavioural Economic study (BE) where post-World War II consumers were coincidently facing a period of unprecedented economic freedom and when the desire for cheap, readily accessible consumable goods really began. As disposable income grew, the High Street emerged from the local shopping parade; the humble convenience store gave way to the supermarket and the observation, collection and analysis of consumer's behaviours developed into a recognisable science.

Throughout this period (one might recognise it is still observable today) if we began to identify the beginning of marketing which 'anchored' products with positive images of celebrities and status, then what of the more subtle and unconscious tactics which began to emerge throughout the 1970s?

We accept the common parlance nowadays, if it is not chosen to be forgotten that our ability to make rational decisions is often unwittingly and cunningly influenced by the 4,000 advertisements we see every day and as long as we do not feel we are being deceived we are willing to 'play along' in this influential romance. We know for example that when we enter a supermarket, the colour, sound, smell, availability and 'convenience' of our goods has been manufactured for us and through marketing and psychological tactics our ability to manage our emotional response is diminished and yet we cheerfully, cooperatively and willingly engage in the joyous deceit day in and day out. We are after all, creatures of habit! This conditioning of a consumer's response to the manufactured stimulus, benefits both the consumer (who joyously engages in the experience and feels unconsciously comforted) and the business - and this is the study and investigation of the Behavioural Economist.

It is within this habitual behaviour of creating 'positive decision responses' for ourselves where the CX professional identifies opportunities to improve the customer experience and where predicting behavioural responses can lead to periods of experimentation and growth for both the business and consumer. As studies into the patterns of consumer behaviour, trends of purchasing bias and emotive decision making are often considered the cornerstone principles of the modern business's psychological marketing strategy, we see behavioural economists influencing popular culture.

Recognising that an increased understanding of the human psyche can support a company's sale of attractive (yet irrational products), is where the psychology gets interesting!

Consider the cover of this book, the title, font and medium by which you are reading this chapter, they have all been chosen specifically to illicit an emotional response within you the reader. Just as Google adjusted the blue font it uses in its hyperlinks to the tone of blue which generated the greatest click-rate and as Amazon adjusted its page-refresh rate to optimize product sales, so too have all the products you have encountered today been designed to create a subconscious emotional response. We encounter and buy products every day whose marketing has affected our perception at our deepest subconscious level and though we might not recognise it, we have filtered the stimulus to determine our emotional response. When a product is advertised, *'just as Mom used to make',* the subtleties become more easily understood as 'Mom's home cooking' provokes an emotional response whether we perceive it or not.

So how do we as CX professionals use this understanding within our roles and how can we identify the patterns of behaviour which can positively impact our customer's decision making?

As anyone who has ever gambled will attest there is a fine line between risk and reward. There exists for many people a tipping point when the emotional brain recognises a risk is too great and the rational decision to withdraw from the game is the right decision to make, but until that point is reached as long as the gambler is not losing too much, the risk is worthwhile.

This understanding of the human bias towards risk and reward is applied in the consumer market as companies who create their branding, product placement and scarcity of resource will identify. Marketing research shows us that creating demand for a product often comes from its perceived availability and those services which appear in high demand are sought after more than those in ready supply (consider 'this year's must have Christmas toy'), whose sales increase when scarcity is created. We see in the marketing of High Street coffee shops the offering of large drinks for similar prices to medium drinks, evoking a sense that for little risk the consumer receives higher reward, though little difference may actually exist. When graphic designers create marketing, branding and advertisement programs, significant investment is made into the psychology of the consumer, whose attention to products is affected by the consumer's values, biases, memories and beliefs. We know from experience that brighter, more colourful branding works best in confectionary and neutral colours work best for baked goods. We see in clothing stores a physical 'path' which directs the consumer to specific items where traffic is highest and that accessories see greater sales when listed towards the end of the customer journey than if provided beside the corresponding item of clothing. Whilst unperceivable to the conscious mind, we make decisions on purchases due to how we feel and it is likely a behavioural economist has influenced the strategy and marketing of the rational and emotional purchases you make.

The practice of creating a positive experience for the customer and one which generates the greatest possible revenue exists when the product matches closely with the consumer's intrinsic beliefs but meets the tipping point between risk and reward. As Coca-Cola found out in 1985, failing to recognise the emotional attachment their consumers had to its branding can lead to disaster, but just the right amount of flex can lead to renewed sales and growth.

In summary, we understand if we look closely at our own biases which products we like and why and with some introspection we can investigate how far from that belief we are willing to stray. Try this new understanding for yourselves: Why did you choose the clothes you are wearing today? Are they the most insulative or durable fabric available, or did you buy them because of how they made you feel? What did you feel when you saw them and why? When you next buy food, do you buy the healthiest products, or are you buying the products whose branding caught your eye, or did they evoke an emotion?

For CX professionals, recognising the *why* is our greatest asset to improve the customer experience and understanding the consumer our greatest skill.

About Richard Jordan

Richard Jordan is a Learning and Development Consultant, Customer Experience expert and the proud Chief Executive of 'Raggit, the Feedback App'; whose mission statement is simply to, "Improve Customer Service".

After a decade in the Royal Marine Commandos and whilst operating as a Sniper in some of the World's harshest environments, Richard identified the importance of empowering, enabling and encouraging people to use their voice for change and created a platform to deliver immediate improvements to the customer's experience.

A highly sought after public speaker, best-selling author and Cultural Enablement coach, Richard is an keen adventurer and Customer Services influencer. To connect with Richard and to follow his exciting journey:

Follow on Instagram, Facebook and Twitter: *@theraggitapp*

Download the Raggit app from the App store today and review individual Customer Service Advisors

It's Not About You, It's About Them

Sirte Pihlaja

How do you create a customer-centric culture? How can you instill that infinite passion you have for customers onto others? Well, the short answer is you can't.

Taking a cruise ship out to sea and encouraging the passengers to have the time of their lives takes more than the bare necessities. It is not enough to provide a life-raft and an umbrella-decorated cocktail with tropical-sounding ingredients.

You need an experienced captain at the helm (leadership), a powerful engine operated with skilful engineers (technology), and meticulously designed customer encounters (processes). In addition, you need operatives (people) who take pride in their work. And teamwork.

Most importantly, for all of these parts to work in perfect unison, and for them to delight your customers, you need a strong company culture.

Piloting your organisational ship is an endeavour unlike any other. None of us wants to end up all Robinson Crusoe'd and left on a desert island. But fear not! Fortunately, there are steps you can take to ease the effort of cultural change on all levels. Taking the five steps outlined in this chapter will help ensure your cultural transformation takes the wind:

1. Define your North Star
2. Chart your course
3. Recruit seasoned sailors
4. Train your crew
5. Empathise, engage and empower

1. Define Your North Star

Building a customer-centric culture always starts from the top. If the captain of your cruise ship doesn't know where they should be taking it, there is little chance anyone else in the organisation will either.

Therefore, the leadership team's responsibility is to define and articulate the North Star for the organisation. This star shines the brightest and leads the sailors in the right direction, even in dark and stormy weather.

People often refer to this North Star as the organisation's Purpose, Vision, or your *Why*. It is the reason behind your organisation's very existence. It tells everyone what you aim to achieve and where you want to go in the future.

"Do we want to be about selling shoes
or do we want to be about something more meaningful?"
— Tony Hsieh, former CEO, Zappos

You should involve your whole leadership team in (re)-thinking this purpose, as well as the possible repercussions future changes may have on your organisational direction, policies and personnel. You will want to be the navigator for this task - hopefully sitting on the board yourself - so you can steer their thinking towards the customer and make her the talk of the day in all future management meetings.

Don't engage the board until you have gathered relevant, up-to-date customer insights. Customer understanding is a critical input to the discussions around the purpose. Otherwise, you will be just guessing.

To ease the cultural shift towards embracing customer-centricity at the top level, you should become best friends with your CFO. They will be a great ally in proving the Return on Investment (ROI) of CX or Return on Experience (RoE), a necessity in winning the leadership team's hearts and minds.

Involving the leaders from the very start is the best way to get them to buy-in and issue a budget for the next steps. Without the top management showing their full commitment and support, your leadership will only give lip-service to your cause.

Committed leaders, on the other hand, will actively participate in creating the CX strategy. They will also help find and fund the right resources to get your CX engines roaring. They will ensure the traction needed for successful training and coaching. They will then start to see the difference their sincere commitment makes to the well-being of the organisation and its employees, and how this follows through in the day-to-day customer operations. They may even help raise the sails if you need to speed up the cultural transformation journey.

Above all, they will demonstrate by their very example, the real importance of these activities to the organisation's future and in getting everyone else on board. Your co-sailors will take note.

2. Chart Your Course

To ensure your ship reaches its destination, you need to chart your route and define your strategy. But not just any strategy! For your employees to deliver great experiences, they will need to have a clear understanding of your customer experience (CX) strategy.

You will need to outline explicitly, what the INTENTIONAL experience is that you want your customers to have and what feelings you want them to enjoy along their journey. These will become the guiding principles for your employees to learn and steer clear of rocks and reefs.

According to the International CEM 2020 Benchmark report, 99% of the organisations who responded want to differentiate through CX, whilst a third admit they don't have a clear CX strategy. Still, 82% say that they have a lot of ongoing CX development. One cannot help but think how much more efficient and profitable these activities could be, if based on a sound CX strategy.

Having a CX strategy also helps you get the resources and budget you need to manage the change. These are two of the most significant barriers to customer-centricity reported in the same study! When your whole leadership team is onboard and preaching about the importance of managing customer experiences, you will not need to worry about other competing business goals getting in the way either.

"In order to empower all employees, it is necessary to align values and vision at all levels."
- Walt Disney, American entrepreneur, animator, writer, voice actor and film producer

Fortunately, charting your course doesn't have to take months and months to achieve. The perfect CX strategy fits on a single sheet of paper, and a first draft can be devised by a few knowledgeable people who are willing and eager to put their best thinking into it.

Defining your CX strategy is a key activity you should not neglect under any circumstances. It is going to be your lifesaver in many storms to come. You also need the CX strategy to easily communicate your thinking to the personnel and help everyone understand their roles in moving in the right direction. Leaders need it to evaluate what skills are necessary to support their team members to achieve these goals.

To create a CX strategy that really resonates - and consequently gets intentionally delivered - you must be intentional when defining it. Always let ideas surface on every level throughout the organisation. Involve as many of your employees in the planning phase as possible. You will reap the rewards later, as the culture gets soaked in.

3. Recruit Seasoned Sailors

To get your cruise ship ready for the sea, you need to decide who will be in charge of the engine room, who keeps the boat neat and tidy (and safely so in these days!) and what passenger care roles you will need to guide, serve and entertain your customers. Likewise, for any CX transformation.

Start by defining your team's roles and responsibilities. You will only want people who clearly understand your customers' and employees' needs and wants.

These teammates must demonstrate a real passion and love for customer experience and employee experience (EX). After all, they enable the cultural shift you want to realise on both the strategic and the operational levels.

"Customers will never love your company until the employees love it first."
- Simon Sinek, Optimist, Founder and Visionary, Simon Sinek Inc.

A CX team should always take an agile approach to development. Getting CX right to stand out is very much about experimenting with new ideas over and over. You will not want to be reactive but proactive, and just like on a ship you have a Master, First Mate, Second Mate, Bosun, Chief Engineer, Second Engineer, Medical Purser, Cook and Watch Leader. There will be many specialist roles to fill in to assist in making business encounters more about the customer.

Recruit seasoned sailors! Remember that these can be people from within your organisation, who are already sitting in the right roles, you just need to team up with them.

In addition to your core team, think ahead and start recruiting cultural ambassadors from within your organisation.

They will play an essential role in driving cultural adoption through in practice, as they can foresee challenges, obstacles and opportunities. They know best what is going on in their part of the organisation and are well-positioned to identify what their team requires to foster new behaviours.

4. Train Your Crew

"Red skies at night, sailors delight. Red sky in the morning, sailors warning." These are simple truths that sailors have come to know as facts through their careers.

Skills required in a job can be trained or acquired through experience. Attitudes, on the other hand, are much harder to teach. If you are in a position to hire new people to your organisation, always hire for attitude.

This is something that Apple has been doing since the beginning. The salesclerks at Apple stores are not tasked with selling, but solving customers' problems. When recruiting, they always look for attitude over IT skills, as the latter can be taught. It is not a coincidence that this determined focus on customer relationships makes customers so loyal to Apple.

"Purpose is like a beacon: it attracts employees who want to work for organisations that they identify with. It also warns off others who may not be the right fit for the company."
- Shaun Smith, Co-founder, Smith+Co

The capability to steer a ship comes from years and years of practice and experience. Your CX ship might only be just leaving the port, but that shouldn't discourage you from starting the journey to a customer-centric culture. Don't despair when you realise that it's not something that people will adopt overnight. An organisational culture takes years to mature.

Vitally, you should involve everyone in the CX development activities and build a culture that inspires them to help each other. Engaged employees create happy customers and save the day when others need a helping hand.

Above everything, make sure that the CX training sessions you invite the organisation to are memorable. After all, the customer experiences your employees will deliver will only be as good as the experiences they remember.

5. Empathise, Engage And Empower

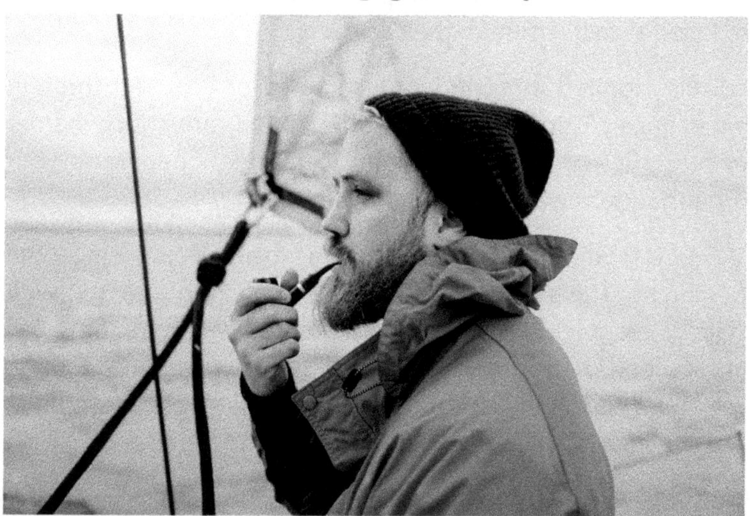

Customer experience belongs to everyone in the organisation. It is not "something the marketing department does". Ultimately, the buck stops with the CEO, but you will not get the results you want if it is not all hands-on deck. In fact, companies should think about their employees before their customers to achieve customer-centricity.

Your customer experiences are a direct reflection of your employee experiences. Happy employees are much more likely to have the energy and desire to deliver happiness to others. So, empathise with your crew to understand where they are coming from. Your job is to be a leader who helps them get to the next level.

Unexpected things may happen even during the most thought-through customer journeys. That's why it makes good (business) sense to empower employees to make decisions independently. Give them the authority to make decisions that can delight or save customers. Most of them will know how to use this power for doing good. Let them follow the North Star.

"We are superior to the competition because we hire employees who work in an environment of belonging and purpose. We foster a climate where the employee can deliver what the customer wants. You cannot deliver what the customer wants by controlling the employee."
- Horst Schulze, Former Ritz Carlton President

Ritz Carlton Hotel has a customer service policy that is a perfect example of employee empowerment. Every employee can spend up to 2 000 USD a day to solve their guests' problems, and they don't need a sign-off from their managers to do the right thing. They can also use this allowance to surprise and delight their customers.

Empowering the staff in this way not only works but also adds to the hotel's perceived mystique, because everyone is trained to be attentive to their guests from their first day at work. What could be your 2K?

A Perfect Storm

Do not try to rush cultural change. Because it's not about you, it's about them. This is about your employees, and it is about your customers. You cannot make anyone love customers. They will have to fall in love themselves.

The journey to customer-centricity takes patience. Every time you feel like giving up, just remember what you are dreaming of achieving - what your North Star is - and you will be in a position to navigate your organisation towards it. But, keep in mind that happiness is a journey, not a destination! Your crew should have a fun, engaging and empowering voyage.

You can, nevertheless, accelerate the transformation by planning the change carefully. Perhaps give it a gentle push by making your own rain and start a perfect storm. Additionally, remember that nobody gets there alone. That is why you must work on all levels and seek support from like-minded people.

Measure your employees' performance and success, be relentless about sharing customer insights, and keep a constant eye on how the culture develops.

Make sure to celebrate what you want the organisational culture to be. Use every occasion to deliver news about positive improvements.

You should be obsessed with where you are going, not with what other companies are doing. Your organisation will need to outperform itself time and over again. Because building a customer-centric culture is a never-ending game. You can always do better. Together.

Sources

- Shirute Ltd. (December 2020). International CEM 2020 Benchmark. https://bit.ly/cem2020-en-results (accessed February 6th, 2021).
- Photos by Tina Rolf and Yiranding on Unsplash
- Photo by cottonbro from Pexels

About Sirte Pihlaja

Sirte Pihlaja (Certified Customer Experience Professional CCXP & LEGO® Serious Play® Trained Facilitator) is the CEO & Customer Experience Optimiser of Shirute, the first customer experience agency in Finland. Sirte is the leader of the global Customer Experience Professionals Association's (CXPA) Finland network and was one of CXPA's founding members and a member of the International Advisory Board. She is one of the first Europeans to have been certified as a CCXP.

Sirte is an internationally known CX/EX expert, coach, designer and strategist with over 25 years of experience advising large international corporations and brands in different industries. She is known for translating customer understanding to concrete actions and results in a fast, fun and cost-efficient way. Sirte was recently recognised as a TOP 150 Global Customer Experience Thought Leader. The CXPA has also awarded her the Extra Mile Award.

Customer Experience 3 is her third book on people experiences. The previous one, *Customer Experience 2*, was a global bestseller on three continents.

Sirte is passionately championing CX in the Nordics, South-East Asia and beyond and is a familiar face in international CX Awards juries and conference stages. She is especially fond of creative methodologies and regularly plays with LEGO bricks together with her clients to create a better future for all of us.

Contacts And Links

LinkedIn: *linkedin.com/in/sirte*

Facebook: *www.facebook.com/shirute*

Instagram: *@sirteace*

Twitter: *@sirteace*

Visit websites:

www.shirute.fi

www.shirute.fi/cem-benchmark

www.cxplay.fi

The Power Of 3Cs: Curiosity, Connections And Commitment - Ingredients To A Flourishing Customer Experience Transformation

Laura Tengerdi

Understanding Yourself Better

I have participated in countless good training programmes over the past two decades but three years ago I had the opportunity to take part on an exceptional one. Not only did it have a unique practical approach on leadership development, but at the end I had to outline my credo. As a customer experience head of a bank, being in the middle of a transformation journey, it could not have come at a better time. I still remember the very last day of the year-long programme when I got the assignment to put together my beliefs within two hours.

Sitting in front of an empty sheet was scary at first, I was not able to write a single word for long minutes, but then it just started flowing. The idea of 3Cs and the meaning behind them was conceived during this process - and, it turned out to be essential for my personal and professional life as well. Also, I believe, these are inevitable for me as a customer experience (CX) specialist.

This chapter is not about sharing the details of my credo, but to emphasise the importance of self-understanding and self-reflection, especially if you want to become an authentic customer officer and also to give you some hints for your transformation journey. What I realised during the years I had been leading the CX transformation at Budapest Bank, Ex-GE Capital, is the fundamental power of Curiosity, Connections and Commitment.

I believe that in order to be able to improve your understanding of your colleagues and customers, first you have to understand yourself and your motivations better.

Now let me show you why this is true by looking at each of the three components:

Curiosity – Listening To People

Why 'Curiosity' is important to me on a personal level?

While outlining my credo I realised that my obsession with CX and its components go back to my teenage years when my psychiatrist mum talked a lot about the importance of curiosity and empathy. Two years ago I accompanied her to the ceremony, which was organised for the 50th anniversary of her becoming a doctor. During the heartwarming event, I was looking at her, asking myself how she could still remember her patients' names and their stories that happened fifty years before. That is because she is phenomenal at active listening - she understands one's thoughts and feelings. My mum has been trying hard since my childhood to teach me this quality. She always says that curiosity keeps you moving forward, because you want to know what comes next. Whenever we talk about this, she likes quoting Einstein: *The important thing is not to stop questioning.*

Einstein, A. (1955) Old Man's Advice to Youth: Never Lose a Holy Curiosity, Life Magazine publication.

Why 'Curiosity' is important to me as a CX leader?

I believe that holding your childlike interest towards your colleagues and customers is of the utmost importance. My dream journey at the bank started five years ago - building a real customer centric culture got on its way with the vision to become the most beloved bank and with the key goal to turn around our NPS from -10.

As a first step we wanted our leadership team to meet real customers so we organised home visits and invited them to participate on focus group discussions. We wanted to make them curious about what our customers say and feel. Then we turned our attention to our employees. We asked whether they would recommend Budapest Bank as a service provider to their friends. To our big surprise, we got lots and lots of answers and as a result we created our CX vision plan. Most importantly we had to pique their curiosity to 'our' cause, by using different methods in the headquarters and in the branches. We introduced a "call a customer" programme for the HQ colleagues, while for our field advisors we organised regional behavioural trainings about how to continuously satisfy and exceed our customers' needs. Getting your colleagues to feel curious and excited is challenging, but rewarding. Curiosity enables empathy and being empathetic help you turn your company into a human-centred organisation.

Encourage your team to talk frequently with colleagues from other departments and most of all meet with your customers. Sit together with your team afterwards and talk about the new insights you all gained during the conversations, and most of all reward them for their curiosity and brave ideas. New experiences put a shine on your personal and professional life.

In my view to be successful in your CX transformation journey you need to regain your childlike curiosity (if you have lost it at some point).

Connections – Getting Everyone Involved

Why 'Connections' are important to me on a personal level?

Being connected is crucial to me: it gives me vitality, makes me more productive and adds meaning to my life. I feel fortunate to have moved to many different cities in Hungary when I was a child, to live in the Netherlands for a short period of time, and later, to travel a lot. Some say that switching homes can be a disruptive experience for a child, but for me moving frequently meant new friends and connections and this made me more open and adaptable. I was 12 years old when I won a Russian translation competition and I had the good fortune to travel to Moscow and Kiev. I travelled alone in a sleeping carriage as part of a totally unknown group and I had to spend the whole time with strangers. During this journey I realised how important it was to make connections easily and it set the course of my life. Since then, I strongly believe in the power of being connected to others both on a professional and a personal level.

Why 'Connections' are important to me as a CX leader?

From the beginning of your CX journey you will find yourself being the 'jack of all trades' - and, being able to connect people easily is a valuable asset for you to move forward on your CX journey.

A lot of people may think that it is only the CX core team's task to make the transformation happen, but it is not true. We CXers are there to help break down silos by connecting people of different departments in cross-functional teams and by defining common goals. In Budapest Bank we created a core team right at the start, including representatives from several key functions, including colleagues from the HQs and also from sales. We followed this principle for our CX decision making committees and for the customer journey meetings as well. These formal meetings help people fall in line and officially connect them to this fluffy sounding topic, but you can reach only 10% of the organisation.

So how will you get everyone on board in the company to your cause? From the employees' perspective, jobs get harder and more insecure so you have to explain clearly what they will gain from it. As an example in Budapest Bank we launched the "Butterfly Effect Experience Days", where we explained the role of employees in building a customer centric culture, the values and relevant behaviours, and the business impact of CX as well. Our 6-pillar CX Maturity Model was the foundation of the Experience Day and connections were made instantly.

We would all like to feel seen and heard and some of us even to be celebrated, so help your teammates to be recognised through the CX programmes. Gather all their initiatives which improved customer satisfaction and use them as good examples in internal communication.

Developing the habit of sharing real customer stories across the whole organization will take your networking to a new level.

Commitment – Doing It Consciously And With Full Heart

Why 'Commitment' is important to me on a personal level?

What brought familiarity in moving across the country as a kid due to my parents changing jobs were the yellow post-it notes. My mum always used them to write positive and engaging messages to me and my sister. My favourite one was the 'nothing is impossible' note, which one day we found posted all over the house, even the bathroom:). Since then this idea drives me - it helps me when I am feeling down, when I am about to start a difficult project or simply when I want to be engaged with something. My mum worked hard to provide a stable foundation for our future and lives her life based on this philosophy. I have learned from her that achieving even the simplest of goals requires us to learn commitment and remain devoted in the pursuit of our goals. We have to find the right motto and it will always guide us on our path.

Why 'Commitment' is important to me as a CX leader?

Your CX journey will have a lot of ups and downs. Sometimes you will be energised and want to move mountains, and sometimes you just want to stop preaching to others about your beliefs. As I have learned from my CX mentor, a global specialist, I.J.Golding: "talking about CX is easy, starting a CX program is hard, but sustaining it in the long term is the hardest."

Commitment from the CEO and the leadership team is a must for a successful programme. It might happen that the initiative comes right from them. That is awesome! Most of the time though, you have to engage leaders for the cause. In the beginning of our journey I borrowed the authority of my mentor, an external specialist and I invited him to talk about the importance of CX.

What helped our senior leaders gain commitment was the launch of a 6-pillar CX Maturity Model. They volunteered to be accountable for the pillars and they helped us in convincing their teams to be part of the culture change. As part of the programme we also achieved that customer related metrics got included in the bonus scheme. As the saying goes: "what gets measured, gets done" - and it is exactly the case when you want others to work for the cause of turning your company into a more customer centric one.

Do not give up even if it feels hard - success requires discipline and dedication. Always keep your goal in mind - if needed use post-it notes for motivation :). When I started the journey in Budapest Bank we chose a vision to become a loveable bank even when people had no trust at all in banking five years after the 2008 crisis. Dare to dream big and devote yourself to the goal - it needs to be high enough to keep you motivated day by day, because for a long time it will be you who has to lead your organisation through the change to become a real customer centric culture.

When your colleagues ask how a project might impact your customers is when you have reached the desired level of commitment.

Final Thoughts – Building Emotional Connection

Dear Reader, whatever you do, make sure you build customer centricity consistently and this will result in a deeper connection to your company and to your brand. Ask yourself: do customers love you? If they do, you are already better than most other players on the market. By being curious about your employees and customers, and systematic in your efforts in making them love your brand, you will create connections your competitors can hardly match. Moreover, the right cause will create buzz in you and in your organisation as well.

I hope you enjoyed this chapter, I just wanted to briefly share with you my philosophy of life, how I found the 3Cs and what I have learned from them to become a better CX Leader. These are the basics of my being and help me stay a passionate professional: Curiosity, Connections and Commitment.

Not everyone of you will become or stay a CX professional. You have to know right at the start if these skills are your friends or your enemies. Whatever you decide to pursue, I hope I could help you a little in your choice.

About Laura Tengerdi CCXP
Brand and Customer Experience Professional, C-Suite, Budapest Bank

Laura Tengerdi has over 25 years of experience in brand marketing and customer experience, managing global and local brands and background in both B2B and B2C roles. She is a big believer of the thought 'customer first', that mindset she mastered during the many years she spent as a senior leader in the Central-European Organisation of Unilever. Later in GE Capital and Budapest Bank she expanded her belief with putting employees in the forefront too. In the last five years she has led the customer experience program for the bank as head of marketing and CX. In 2018 she became the 1st CCXP (Certified Customer Experience Professional) in CEE.

Listed among the 50 most successful marketing professionals in Hungary (Marketing&Media) and was shortlisted for the CX Leader of the Year 2020, globally (MyCustomer.com). Talks frequently at marketing and CX conferences and takes part on CX award ceremonies as a judge.

Contacts And Links

Email: *lauratengerdi@gmail.com*

Linkedin: *https://www.linkedin.com/in/laura-tengerdi-ccxp*

Bringing The Fun Out Of The CX Function: Engage Employees And Activate A Customer-Centric Culture

Stephanie Linville

"What we learn with pleasure we never forget."
Alfred Mercier

As the Customer Experience (CX) discipline evolves, the link between CX and Employee Experience (EX) is increasingly viewed as an inextricable one. The return on investment of any CX program is achieved when employees understand customers' needs and expectations, and they can take action aligning their roles and behaviors with those requirements to eliminate pain points. Leading organizations with mature CX programs incorporate dynamic approaches to capturing, analyzing, prioritizing, and implementing Voice of the Customer (VOC) feedback. These organizations also provide effective tools and resources to engage and develop their employees to nurture an organizational culture that successfully puts the customer at the center of designing and delivering exceptional experiences.

But how can organizations, large and small alike, create the types of customer-centric cultures needed to compete in today's rapidly changing environment?

In this chapter, you will discover how to use gamification to make fun, yet meaningful, connections between your CX work and the way employees view their roles in the organization to serve customers and drive true loyalty.

What Science Tells Us About The Connection Between Fun, Learning, And Employee Engagement

In her recent book, *Research-Based Strategies to Ignite Student Learning*, neurologist Judy Willis found fun experiences increase levels of dopamine, endorphins, and oxygen – all things that promote learning.[1] A study titled *Does fun promote learning? The relationship between fun in the workplace and informal learning* published in the Journal of Vocational Behaviour showed informal learning is important for employees to learn the skills needed to improve their work. The study also identified employees are more likely to try new things if their work environment is fun. However, it is important to note the study concluded that the 'fun' is not as important as the environment created to facilitate learning.[2]

Since fun experiences enable people to learn better and try new things, organizations should view playful work activities as an effective way to drive employee engagement and foster a culture of creativity and innovation, rather than a disruption to the normal routine or a frivolous expenditure of organizational time and resources. The study above also found positive connections between fun, employee performance, and retention. In addition, fun activities increase employee resilience and optimism, which in turn leads to better attention on tasks.[2] All of those outcomes have positive, long-term impacts on an organization's bottom line.

Now that the link between fun and employee learning and overall engagement has been established, let us extrapolate this idea to the CX discipline.

Using Gamification In CX Programs To Engage Employees

Gamification has become quite the buzzword during the past several years because many brands have achieved success by incorporating gamification into some of their CX and EX strategies. These strategies are effective, because gamification evokes positive player emotions such as curiosity, happiness, and excitement, and these positive experiences lead to increased engagement and loyalty.

To clarify, gamification is defined as a set of activities and processes to solve problems by using or applying the characteristics of game elements.[3] As CX professionals, we are all trying to solve how to engage employees and activate a customer-centric culture. When I talk about gamifying CX insights, I am not referring to some sort of points programs used to drive specific loyalty behaviors. Rather, I am talking about using game thinking and elements of game design to engage employees in fun activities, so they learn about the customer experience and gain a deeper understanding of the customers they serve and support.

Here are some actionable examples with which I have successfully gamified elements of CX programs using concepts from popular TV game shows and classic board games to increase employee engagement and activate a customer-centric culture:

Gamification of VOC insights – Family Feud

One hundred customers surveyed.
Their top eight answers are on the board.
What do customers say is our company's biggest strength?

1	5
2	6
3	7
4	8

- **Background:** One of the great things about Family Feud is its universal appeal. Not only is the concept simple (i.e., guess the most popular answers to basic survey questions given by respondents), but the game show has been around for decades. It first aired in the United States in 1976 and has aired or is currently airing in over 70 countries.[4]
- **Objective:** For employees to gain a deeper understanding of your customers and the overall experience they have with your organization.
- **Audience:** This game allows participation across all levels of an organization.
- **How to Play:** The format of this game can be customized based on the size and structure of the organization. Teams should consist of three to five players each and can be aligned functionally or cross-functionally. There can be any number of teams, but for each round, two teams compete by giving what they think are the top responses given by customers to VOC and/or market research survey questions. Points are proportionally given to the answers with the highest frequency of mention. Whichever team gets the most points advances to the next round, and the game continues until there is only one team remaining. While this team might have won the game, all players are winners, because they come away with more CX knowledge.
- **Outcomes Achieved:** This is a fun game and almost always elicits a sense of friendly competition among teams. Hopefully, you will hear exciting feedback like, "I learned something new today!" or "I knew more about our customers than I thought I did!"
- **Additional Things to Consider:** Some possible questions to include in your game might be 'why do customers choose your company/brand?' Or 'what do customers say are your business' opportunities for improvement?' Include questions that are not too obvious but are not extremely challenging or require detailed knowledge about a specific functional area. Also, avoid topics that highlight any one group or team in a negative light.

Remember the point of the game is for employees to have fun and learn something new about your customers and the experience they have with your organization.

Gamification of the Customer Journey – Chutes and Ladders (also known as Snakes and Ladders)

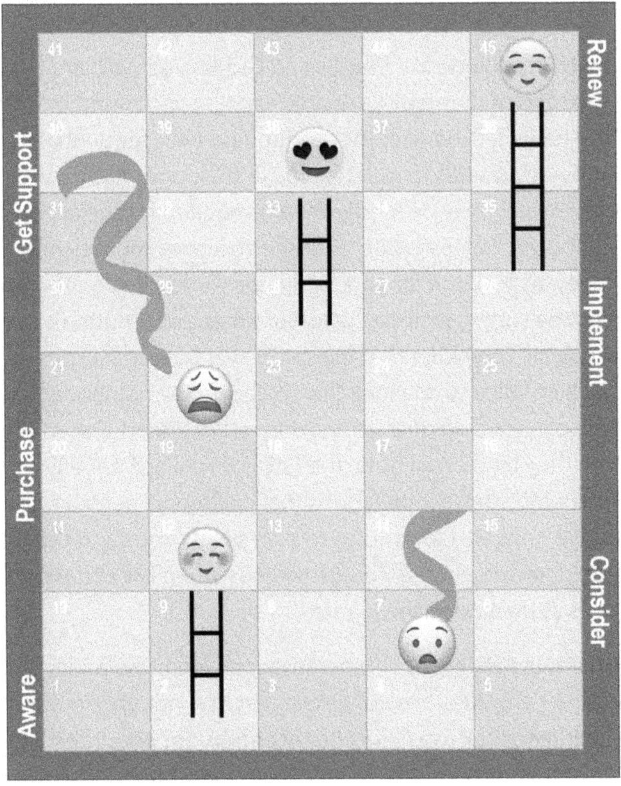

- **Background:** This is a classic board game and a favorite of children around the world, so your employees should be familiar with this. It has been speculated this game has been played in India since the 2nd century AD. It was introduced to Great Britain by India's colonial rulers towards the end of the 19th century and became known as Snakes and Ladders. The game then traveled to the United States where in 1943 it was launched by Milton Bradley as Chutes and Ladders.[5]

- **Objective:** For employees to gain knowledge of the customer journey stages as well as the customer goals, emotions, and the key "Moments That Matter" associated with each stage of the journey.

- **Audience:** This game is best suited for two to four players at a time within a specific functional group. Players will benefit the most when the journeys or micro-journeys are related to their roles.

- **How to Play:** A typical Chutes and Ladders gameboard consists of ten rows of numbered squares, starting with number one in the lower left-hand corner continuing with sequentially numbered squares to number 100 in the upper right-hand corner, which may be longer than is required for these purposes. Develop your game board to fit the customer journey or micro-journey and tailor it for your audience. As you design the game board, be sure to include customer goals and emotions and identify all "Moments That Matter." Players can use a spinner or a pair of dice to advance their piece on the gameboard. When players land on a ladder, they move ahead. Conversely, when they land on a chute, they slide backward. Labeling the ladders with those interactions that customers perceive as positive ones and the chutes as pain points adds additional context for the players. The game ends when the first person arrives at the end of the journey.

- **Outcomes Achieved:** This game can be effective in increasing customer empathy among employees. It is not uncommon to hear feedback like, "I had not ever thought about the impact our contract process has on our customers, but I can see why that would be frustrating."

- **Things to Consider:** In advance of the game, share a version at their own pace. As part of the game activities, share success stories highlighting the customer journey by sharing audio or video recordings from customer interactions, or better yet bring in customers to share their positive experience directly with the employees.

Gamification of Customer Personas – Guess Who?

- **Background:** Guess Who? is a character-guessing game first manufactured by Milton Bradley in 1979 and is now owned by Hasbro.[6]
- **Objective:** For employees to understand the characteristics, goals, motivations, and pain points of each customer persona.
- **Audience:** This game is best suited for employees who are in the same functional area and have customer-facing roles, e.g., sales representatives, marketing professionals, or contact center employees. This game is ideal for new employee onboarding, sales enablement workshops, and other training and development activities.
- **How to Play:** This can be played in pairs or with two teams. Each player or team receives a customer persona to review before starting the game. Each player or team takes turns asking the opponent a 'Yes' or 'No' question about their mystery persona. The goal of the game is to guess who your opponent's persona is before they guess yours. Be sure to include all the relevant customer information on the personas (e.g., age, marital status and children, job title and responsibilities, goals, informational sources, decision-making needs, key messaging, technology comfort level, knowledge of your business and processes, challenges, and pain points).
- **Outcomes Achieved:** Like the journey map example, this game is effective in evoking customer empathy in employees. After using this game in a sales enablement workshop, a seasoned sales representative sent me this feedback, "After that session, I applied what I learned to my next sales presentation. The customized talking points provided in the customer personas really enhanced my delivery."

- **Things to Consider:** Design the personas used in this game so that employees will be able to keep them visible in their workspaces. Seeing the personas every day will help employees keep customers' needs, motivations, and pain points top of mind.

A Last Word – Activating A CX Culture With Remote Employees

With more employees working virtually, it is important to consider the needs of remote employees as you design your CX culture activation strategies. These gamification ideas can prove to be an effective way to engage your employees whether they are working in an office, remotely, or some hybrid of these two scenarios.

Also, there has been a recent explosion of technological capabilities aimed at fostering collaboration across remote teams. Use these tools and platforms to bring together employee groups, unlock the fun in your work, and watch how the innovation and creativity that transpires can deliver outstanding customer experiences.

I hope this chapter sparks creativity into your CX program and inspires you to use similar or other creative gamification techniques to instill a deep customer knowledge across your organization. As my kids always tell me, the fun only stops if you let it!

References

1. Judy Willis, Research-Based Strategies to Ignite Student Learning (ASCD 2020)

2. Michael Tewis, "Does fun promote learning? The relationship between fun in the workplace and informal learning" (2017) Volume 98, Journal of Vocational Behavior, Pages 46-55

3. 'Gamification', Merriam Webster [website] [no date] <www.merriam-webster.com/dictionary/gamification>, accessed 11 February 2021

4. Mark Goodson, 'Family Feud International', Fandom [website], [no date] <www.markgoodson.fandom.com/wiki/Family_Feud/International>, accessed 12 February 2021

5. Wu Mingren, 'The Origin of Snakes and Ladders: A Moral Guide of Vice and Virtue', Ancient Origins [website], 7 May 2018, <www.ancient-origins.net/history-ancient-traditions/origin-snakes-and-ladders-moral-guide-vice-and-virtue-0010012>, accessed 12 February 2021

6. 'Guess Who?', Wikipedia [website] [no date] <www.en.wikipedia.org/wiki/Guess_Who%3F>, accessed 12 February 2021

About Stephanie Linville

Stephanie Linville is a Certified CX Professional (CCXP) with over 20 years of experience on both sides of the CX discipline – provider and practitioner. She is known for her creativity and entrepreneurial spirit and has worked in a variety of industries throughout her career, including financial services, SaaS, education, transportation, healthcare, retail, and consumer goods. She has a passion for elevating the Voice of the Customer and activating market and customer insights across all functions of an organization to design exceptional experiences, drive employee engagement, and positively impact business outcomes.

Stephanie is active member in Customer Experience Professionals Association (CXPA), and in 2017, she earned its CX Impact Award for Outstanding Practitioner which recognizes her leadership of organizational CX efforts and inspiring excellence in all aspects of the CX discipline.

She has a personal goal of appearing on Family Feud with her husband, Brad (who is also a CCXP), and their three adult children: Rachel, Zack, and Sophie. Connect with her on social media to share more fun and engaging CX best practices.

Contacts and Links

LinkedIn: *https://www.linkedin.com/in/stephanie-linville*

Twitter: *@StephLinville*

Disney Employee Experience: Tangible Examples Of How To Engage Employees And Why You Should

Francesca Tempestini

Why should you care about employees? Because they are the ones who take care of your customers.

Many companies believe in the importance of having their own employees engaged and providing them with great experiences; as a former Cast Member of Disneyland Paris, I had the chance to live and benefit from this approach, which walks hand in hand with the principles of Employee Experience (EX). Employee Experience is the sum of all interactions that an employee has with her employer during the duration of their working relation.[1] EX is relevant for the success of a business because it is directly connected to the way customers feel about a company: happy employees means happy customers.[2]

My purpose in this chapter is to reflect on what it meant for me to be a Cast Member in the light of EX and identify a few examples of Employee Engagement. I am not spilling the beans on all the ways you can engage employees; I just would like to call out the most important and easy ones to replicate.[3]

Company Culture

"If you don't know where you want to go,
then it doesn't matter which path you take."[4]

When you start at the top, it is tough to adjust to average. Bearing this in mind, today I can state beginning my working career as a Cast Member has been the best thing that could have happened to me. And also, the worst.

Disney set the bar extremely high, and as soon as I left, I knew finding another job where I felt as good as I did there was not going to be easy. And I was right. For a longtime I thought if I wanted to be happy at work, I should either go back to Disney or work for Zappos or Apple. Today I know that any company can have a Disney-like working environment and transform the way it is perceived by customers and employees by applying the principles of Customer Experience (CX) and Employee Experience.[5]

A point often raised when I mention Employee Experience is: if a person is paid to do a job, he or she must perform it to the best of his or her ability. Wrong! Paying someone is only the starting point - a 'bare necessity'. Motivating a person, engaging her, having her walk the extra-mile, is another story. "First impressions are strong and lasting ones. But customers are not the only people who get fast and firm first impressions, so do employees".[6]

Employees are part of the equation for your business success. They need to know what you want them to do, how you want them to do it and why. And how would they know all of that? Company culture.

I arrived at Disneyland Paris, France, in 2007. During the first two days I attended an orientation called Traditions: I was given an overview of company history from Walt Disney's birth through the evolution of The Walt Disney Company. I learned the values of The Company, the rules, everything they expected from me and what I could expect from them. Shared values, goals, attitudes, practices... this - and much more- is company culture. It feels good when everything is said right from the beginning; as a new employee, I felt a sense of trust because everything was crystal clear. If you don't set and explain the rules, you cannot pretend anyone follows them; they are not instantly downloaded in employees' minds when they sign the contract.

Company culture is "the way people feel about the work they do, the values they believe in, where they see the company going and what they're doing to get it there".[7] After Traditions, I wanted to be there, I wanted to be part of that world. The First thing you need to do to engage your employees is establish a company culture: set rules.

Motivation

"Ohana means family, and family means no one is left behind or forgotten."[8]

When it comes to motivation, everyone is different. Companies, however, have tools like journey mapping[9] which help determine touchpoints with customers and employees. Drawing an Employee Journey Map can help an organization determine the best strategy to make sure motivation occurs during all the stages of an employee lifecycle.[10]

Onboarding is one of the first touchpoints a company has with employees. Before my arrival to Disney, I received a welcome letter with many useful information, especially considering I was moving to France from Italy: how to get from airport to campus, how to get my security number and what doctors were around the corner etc. There is always pertinent information you can share with newcomers. In my first job after Disney, which was a 45 minute drive from home, I would have appreciated knowing I should grab my lunch on my way there because I was literally in the middle of nowhere and I would lose a lot of time going to the nearest town; it would have also been good to know I better not park in a certain spot because it was a neighbor's private property, even though there was no sign. When you are the last to arrive, these little details help you feel looked after and can save you some trouble.

Motivation passes through communication. Being able to provide feedback and been heard when something goes wrong, increases employees motivation. Early in my Disney career, I was assigned to a certain team for five months. From day one my new team sent me to help other locations, without training me first. I hated it: instead of being helpful, I was feeling embarrassed because I was making mistakes since I had little knowledge of the job. I went to see the manager, I explained how bad this situation was for everyone: the teams I was sent to were expecting to be helped, I expected to be trained and my own team expected to be thanked. None of this was happening. A solution was set: I would receive a little training first and be sent to other locations later. Provide direct feedback to a supervisor about a decision; be heard; be given the right tools to perform your tasks: these are powerful motivators.

I do agree with Lisa Lai who suggest another way to consider motivation: focusing less on employees doing great work and more about employees feeling great about their work.[11] In this regard, people's attitude around you is a motivator too. At Disney, I appreciated the fact that company rules and values were followed by everyone. I do remember vividly how all Senior Managers would stroll the park picking up trash from the floor on their way because our common goal was having a neat and clean park, and everyone contributed.

Set rules, provide tools; lead by example.

Value Your Employees

"Sometimes the smallest things take up the most room in your heart." [12]

At Disney, Cast Members are valued in multiple ways. It might be a guest who leaves a word of appreciation for someone, or fellow cast members who nominates a colleague who inspires them by being a real example of Disney values. Rewards are given to entire teams and to individuals. Awards and recognitions are shared to celebrate, inspire, and to create that company culture we talked about, which is all about working together for the same goal, going in the same direction and taking pride in the good work of everyone.

You don't have to set up a big event in order to make employees feel valued; a nice word is a good start. A couple of months after I started working in Guest Relations, I was happily surprised when a Team Leader came to me inquiring how I was doing and if I needed anything. She made a point of telling me all my supervisors were happy with my performance and the entire team was glad to have me onboard. The effect that a short conversation had on me was incredible: it boosted my morale and made me want to go above and beyond. That year I was awarded for the number of times guests left an appreciation note for my work.

It is important to show employees they are valued, especially when something goes wrong. The annual evaluation can be a solid moment of growth when goals are set, strong and weak points are shared with the intent to work on them - not to blame. You can't find the perfect employee, but you can help a good employee improve herself. In one of my post-Disney jobs, evaluation turned out to be a big de-motivator when I realised it was just a list of 'not good' without any active listening or goal setting: "The problem is not the problem. The problem is your attitude about the problem".[13]

Set rules, provide tools; lead by example. Reward.

Working Environment

"The secret, Alice, is to surround yourself with people who make your heart smile. It's then, only then, that you'll find Wonderland."[14]

Employee Engagement is much more than what I have been writing about. Sharing information, involving employees in company decisions and procedure-making, giving them the right tools, allowing them to have a work-life balance, empowering them. The list goes on. At the center of all of this, there is A person.

Employees can be your greatest Heroes or greatest Villains. It is not a question of giving them more money; it is a matter of them feeling part of a team, engaged, involved and dedicated. You cannot order a person into being dedicated - you need to structure your organization in such a way that your people will be proud to be YOUR people.

I believe having a great workplace where employees are happy is not an unachievable utopia nor Disneytopia requiring pixie dust - which is indeed rather difficult to gather out in the market. There are some elements which are absolutely available to every company wanting to achieve that. But what we should not forget, is we are all humans. Customers, leaders, employees; we all want to be heard, considered, feel we belong to something, and that we matter. People matter.

As Walt Disney said: " You can design and create and built the most wonderful place in the world. But it takes PEOPLE to make the dream a reality".[15]

References

1. Franz, A. Customer Understanding: Three Ways to Put the 'Customer' in Customer Experience (and at the Heart of Your Business), 2019, p.36

2. Stolpe, M. 'What Is Employee Experience and How Is It Different From Engagement?', Bonfyre, [blog], <https://bonfyreapp.com/blog/what-is-employee-experience> last accessed 15 Feb.2021

3. For a deeper insight: Franz A. 'How do we ensure employees are happy?', CX Journey [blogspot](7 March 2018) < https://cx-journey.com/2018/03/how-do-we-ensure-employees-are-happy.html>, last accessed 15Feb 2021

4. Geronimi C., Jackson W., Luske H. (dirs.), Alice in Wonderland (RKO Radio Pictures/Walt Disney Productions, 1951)

5. The Disney Institute trains executives of different industries to the Disney Approach since 1996 (www.disneyinstitute.com).

6. Be Our Guest: Perfecting the Art of Customer Service, Disney Institute (New York: Disney Editions, 2003), p. 75

7. 'Understanding Company Culture', Built In [website], <https://builtin.com/company-culture> last accessed 15 Feb. 2021.

8. Sanders C., DeBlois D. (dirs.), Lilo and Stitch (Buena Vista Pictures Distribution, Inc./Walt Disney Feature Animations, 2002)

9. More about Journey Mapping: Franz, A. Customer Understanding: Three Ways to Put the 'Customer' in Customer Experience (and at the Heart of Your Business), p36. 2019

10. More about employee lifecycle: Franz, A. 'Employee Experience Lifecycle', CX Journey [blogspot] (22 Dec. 2011), <https://cxjourney.blogspot.com/2011/12/employee-experience-lifecycle.html?m=1>, last accessed 15 Feb 2021.

11. Lai, L. 'Motivating Employees Is Not About Carrots or Sticks', Harvard Business Review [website], (June 2017)

<https://hbr-org.cdn.ampproject.org/c/s/hbr.org/amp/2017/06/motivating-employees-is-not-about-carrots-or-sticks.>
Last accessed 15 Feb. 2021.

12. Lounsbery J., Reitherman W. (dirs), The Many Adventures of Winnie the Pooh (Buena Vista Distributions/Walt Disney Production, 1977)

13. Verbinski G., Brukheimer J. (dirs), Pirates of the Caribbean: The Curse of the Black Pearl (Buena Vista Pictures Distributions/ Walt Disney Pictures, 2003)

14. Geronimi C., Jackson W., Luske H. (dirs.), Alice in Wonderland (RKO Radio Pictures/Walt Disney Productions, 1951)

15. Walt Disney Famous Quotes (Disney Kingdom Editions, 1994), p.80

About Francesca Tempestini

Francesca is an enthusiastic disseminator of the Disney Approach and a Customer Experience lover.

She spent five years as a Cast Member in Disneyland Paris where she worked mainly in the departments of Guest Relations and Guest Care. She has ten years experience in the B2B sector, mainly in the role of Export Manager in the glass industry.

Francesca likes to combine her Disney experience with CX and EX principles, bringing Disney sparkles and insights to non-magical industries. Her goal is to show how the Disney Approach can be applied to any industry, promoting a people-centric approach to business which includes employees.

In 2020 she has been hosted by Gregorio Uglioni CCXP on his CX Goalkeeper Podcast, giving insights of Employee and Customer Experience in Disneyland Paris. In the same year, she has been Guest Lecturer at the Universal University of Moscow, giving much appreciated lectures on "Company Communication: the Disney example" and "Business Ethics and Corporate Responsibility: a Disney perspective".

Contacts And Links

www.linkedin.com/in/francesca-tempestini-CX

2. Organisation Adoption And Accountability

Having clear priorities and accountability in an continuous improvement environment

Eat Your Own Dog Food

Sharon Boyd

When did you last shop your own shop?

Previously, I worked for a retail chain and overheard one of my senior colleagues say that they weren't the target demographic for our brand, and so they never shop with us. I have a very limited poker face and remember being a bit shocked by the way they said it. It was incredibly smug and snooty, and made me want to hit him. That moment really sharpened my focus - it has always made me wonder how you can make valid decisions that affect the future of a business, employees and customers if you don't understand or ahem... actually experience your customer experience?! Answer; you can't.

I'm not just 'talking shop' here, excuse the pun; when did you last dine at your own restaurant, book into your own garage, or 'eat your own dog food'?! Obviously, I don't expect you to do the last one on the list, literally, but you get the idea.

This should be the simplest, most obvious point in the book. Yet so many people (leaders in particular), shy away from it. Assuming they know the customer journey as they've been in the company for 18 years. Okay, but have you ever ordered anything from your website? Called your helpdesk out of hours? Tried to use the chat function? If not, how can you possibly gauge first-hand whether your CX is any good?

The Why

I could list a million different reasons why we should test our own CX. Firstly, we get to rub elbows amongst our customers, if it's an 'in real life' situation (I so appreciate what that phase means, since the pandemic!). We see their body language as they queue. Their expressions as they pay or when they complain, when they clock our prices, or when they are greeted by our staff. But just as valid, is when our customer facing teams are remote from the customer. I've seen some shocking baton passes recently. Ones that just stop abruptly, with a full-on baton drop.

We are also able to feel the customer's joy, and the discomfort, just as they do. I can't tell you the volume of projects that have rocketed to the top of the funding list, after a senior leader has spoken to a customer directly, had a family member complain or felt the customer's pain themselves. Suddenly… sh*t gets done!!

It's not just for leaders though. It's agonisingly obvious, when we ring a helpline for assistance, and it is clear that the agent does not have a clue how to navigate through the system they are meant to be guiding us through. Every, single, customer facing agent should have completed the steps of a process that a customer has to complete, if they are supporting that customer process. Again, it's obvious. Right?

IF YOU DON'T EAT YOUR OWN 'DOG FOOD', HOW DO YOU EXPECT TO KNOW IF IT'S ANY GOOD?

MKL

MKL CX

So why is there so much pain and resistance around 'back to the floor' days etc? A select few embrace it. They learn how to use the tills. To drive the vans. To pick the items. Take calls. Others stand about taking bored selfies. They simply don't see the value.

I am actually writing this in a car garage. I've just been told by the garage owner how he has a super rare motor bike - only six in the country. That he uses his own mechanic to service his bike, as he absolutely trusts him (he then introduced me to said mechanic, who was working on my own pride and joy). As a customer sitting here watching his operation, I am very reassured by this. This is not a swanky garage, far from it. It's cluttered, the sofas are ripped and it could do with some TLC, but so far I've been offered the WIFI and a cuppa, I'm loving hearing about his passion for vehicles, and I can't help but listen to his smile as he chats to his customers on the phone. This guy is at the coalface, and he is owning it!! Not just that, he has changed this particular customer from a 'new customer' to 'returning customer'.

There Is Always A Way

What happens if it is a service you don't need as an individual? It's something aimed at industry or commercial?

Or what if you provide patient care? Obviously, you can't become a patient just to test out your own patient journey.

Okay let's pause. What we did in the last few sentences was just come up with excuses. There is ALWAYS a way to shop your own shop. Even if you get allll the way to the moment of no return and stop. We can park in the patient car park. We can check out the patient comms. We can try the patient food (for those of you who have gone through labour, how amazing is your first meal and first shower? Wouldn't it be amazing if they were at least adequate for what we have just been through?!). Food, in any experience, is not to be overlooked! (Airlines take note).

At MKL, we provide commercial Internet of Things solutions as part of our offering. Not something I need particularly in my own house. But there are a lot of aspects of what we offer, that I can test out. Our automated customer comms from our software, the engineer on-site visit, or our cheerful greetings on the helpline, to name just a few!

If you REALLY can't live your own experience, then you can do the next best thing. Simulate.

IF YOU CAN'T FULLY EXPERIENCE THE WHOLE CUSTOMER JOURNEY FIRST-HAND, IMMERSE YOURSELF WHERE YOU CAN AND SIMULATE THE REST.

MKL CX

At MKL, we run 'white pumpkin' events where companies come and simulate the complete customer journey, offsite with us. This works especially well if you are changing or creating a new customer proposition. Those delivering the service play out the interactions with basic props (least number of distractions as possible) so we can have a good hard look at how everything runs, and really put ourselves in the customer's shoes. When the leadership join in (rather than just observe), either as the 'customer' or as the 'provider' role - it works a million times better. Being offsite, allows everyone to completely immerse themselves and clearly hear the customer voice. We journey map at the same time, video where it adds value, and then we watch the whole thing back with the map and ask what everyone learned, and how they are going to simplify, add consistency and increase delight.

It's a valuable day out, but the key value comes afterwards. Our businesses live and die by the standard of our customer experiences, so after we've had a good sniff, kicked the tyres, taken our operation for a whirl; what we do next is vital.

So What Next?

So - you've eaten your own dog food. If you loved the taste - wow congratulations! Now you need all your team to eat it too. To become real advocates. We all know how much easier it is to 'sell' a product if we believe in it. Customers can feel sincerity. So, get your team touching, feeling, eating (if appropriate!!) your products and services. Make sure it is accessible to all of them. If that is free tickets/reservations/discounts etc., then get it done.

Protect it. Keep it current. Ensure that decisions aren't made to the detriment of your customer experience.

Or maybe you've tasted the dog food and it wasn't so hot? Okay, so now we know. Now we can fix it.

What Else Can We Do?

We go have a good sniff about elsewhere. What's out there? What is that other airline doing? Why is that hairdressers ALWAYS booked up for weeks when ours isn't? Why do people still go to that MOT place even though its wayyyy shabbier than ours? Don't read about them, go and see for yourself.

Ask your teams. What AMAZING experiences have our teams felt in our sector, that we don't do?

I mentioned in the CX2 book about Gemba walks. Seeing your experience in situ. DO IT!!

Eating your own dog food is not a one off. It is a MINDSET. If we want to be leaders worth our salt, we need to be so invested in our offering that we really know it. We know what will impact it and how. Not to be too cringy, but we need to have our finger on the pulse of the customer facing business. Which means go and shop your shop!!

However. Do it right. One of things I hate most is when a leader calls ahead for a 'visit'. I have witnessed this so many times! All leave is cancelled. The operation is overstaffed, leaving the rest of the week on skeleton staff (awful CX for the rest of the week then...). Everyone is on their best behaviour. The site has been primped and plumped.

The 'guest' arrives, sweeps around and leaves feeling good that they have 'checked in'. All is gooooood in the hood. Except it's not. It's not a real representation of the operation. It's certainly not what your customers are getting every day.

We should not be a 'guest' in our own operations. We should be part of the furniture! A piece of furniture who is part of the team. Who notices that the delivery arrives late every day, and quietly rings the supplier and sorts it. Who sees that the duty manager is juggling, trying to blow up balloons for a party, deal with a complaint, and taking two bookings, so takes over the balloon pumping. This is how we really know what is going on. This is how we really understand the customer experience. AND we get to see the employee experience too. First-hand. We are one! We are not a 'guest'. And whilst I'm at it - please don't turn up all suited and booted if your team wears casual. Again, we are there to be part of the team.

Nothing I've said here is rocket science. But why do we see so little of the management working out in our chains? I can work just as well in a garage as I can in the office, I've proved that today. In fact, I've been inspired.

So...tell me about your 'dog food'. Is it the best it can be? Every time? Would you eat it?

If not, you know what to do!

About Sharon Boyd

Sharon Boyd is MD for MKL CX and Chief Customer Officer (CXO) at MKL Innovation. MKL is a CX and Tech company that specialises in transformational technology – especially around sustainability and operational efficiency. MKL have centred their entire business completely around the customer, with a heavy focus on making everything as easy as possible.

Sharon was voted inside the top 25 UK top CX Influencers (CXM magazine) in 2021. She has been a captain of the CX World Games (returning again this year... CX Innovators to win!), a finalist at Customer Centricity World Series 2021, a CX judge at the UK CX Awards 2020, and is a Director at the Customer Institute.

She has recently completed her MBA at Cranfield University, and is a fully qualified Programme Manager, a Lean Six Sigma Green Belt, Certified Patient Experience Practitioner and a Certified Customer Experience Professional.

Sharon has over twenty years of experience in customer facing operations with technical knowledge, proven delivery and a strong customer focus. Having delivered multi-million-pound programmes for several blue-chip companies across retail, hospitality, IT, telecoms and aviation, she brings a well-rounded and strategic approach.

Connect with Sharon for coaching, CX/EX projects or a good ol' CX in Tech geek-out!

Contacts And Links

Sharon@MKLCX.co.uk

www.MKLInnovation.com

www.MKLCX.co.uk

www.linkedin.com/in/boydlsharon
and *https://www.linkedin.com/company/mklcx*

Instagram *@mkl_cx_arm*

Twitter *@MKLCustomerExp*

CX Governance: Orchestrating The Organization's Tempo

Mohamad El-Hinnawi

The focus on customer experience as a strategic competitive advantage has been growing at a fast pace in organizations over the last decade. A recent research by NTT[1] shows that 81.6% of organizations agree that CX offers a competitive edge and 58% say it's their primary differentiator, yet it forms a crucial part of organizational strategy for just 14.4%. Also, only 26.2% of the respondents say that the value of CX is fully defined and tracked.

As CX professionals, I believe most of us relate to the above. We are able to see this whether in our organizations or when we are customers of others. In fact, I find myself always wearing the hat of a CX consultant as I evaluate the experience delivered to me, not in terms of how it is delivered, but rather in terms of the root causes that make it delivered to me as such.

Over the last few months, and with the implications of COVID, I have been ordering items online more than ever. As I was attracted to the solid branding, diversity of products, and the quick delivery times of one of the eCommerce platforms, I started ordering items on a weekly basis. It initially started with a smooth experience where I selected my products, placed them in the cart, effortlessly added my shipping address through the location services, and paid through Apple Pay.

Bingo! My items were delivered in no time.

As this was a great experience, I started ordering more and more from this company. With time, I started receiving calls from the company asking me to verify my address before each and every delivery.

What was once a great experience is now a nightmare!

The least of my expectations would be for an eCommerce company to contact me via phone to validate my address that is already captured via their location services – and even worse – after my items have been successfully delivered to my address more than 15 times already.

What also adds to the pain is the way the calls are handled. Some of the agents sound more robotic than robots, sticking to their script and speaking over me. Other agents that had some basic human and service skills kept on apologizing when I tell them I am so annoyed with the calls, and they claim that they raised a complaint. Sure enough, calls keep on coming at nine in the morning every time I have an expected delivery.

What comes to my mind right away is the lack of alignment within the company. Disconnected teams and processes, lack of proper utilization of the technology – though digital is at the core of eCommerce value proposition - and lack of action on complaints. While the company planned to improve its field operations, it has created a consistent negative experience that could have been avoided have the company adopted an approach of collaborative design.

Looking at the matter from an internal perspective, and as I have been involved in assessing the CX maturity of several organizations, I cannot but reflect on the observation that in almost every organization I engaged with, the least level of engagement with the customer centric initiatives was noticed at the level of middle management.

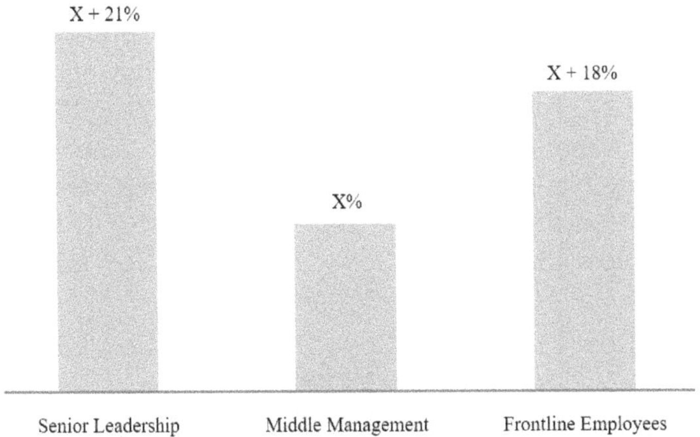

Figure 1 – Percentage of buy-in towards CX initiatives
© 2021 Mohamad El-Hinnawi

Following those findings, and looking further into the gathered insights, it turns out that the reason for senior leadership's buy-in is that by nature, senior leaders cope well with the emerging fields in business, and accordingly; customer centricity pretty much becomes a common dimension in corporate strategies nowadays. Front-liners develop a certain level of empathy that makes them buy-in into CX initiatives more than other players in the organization since they are naturally closer to customers' pains and challenges.

The main cause for lack of buy-in at the level of middle management, is the lack of aligning the operational KPIs of middle managers with the overarching strategic objectives. Some might think that this is a result of poor empowerment, whereas it seems to be more of a governance and alignment issue. In this sense, we are not talking about alignment of a core CX team and its setup and relevant KPIs only, but about a fully functional governance that defines the proper interactions, objectives, delivery and other important aspects related to the CX initiatives across the organization.

The lack of alignment was also highlighted in the 2020 Customer Experience Benchmarking report done by NTT, where 66.6% (was 53.4% in 2019) of organizations said they don't apply an aligned CX strategy across the enterprise. Of these, 37.3% define their strategies individually and 29.3% say CX is relevant only in some business functions. In the insights, the study highlights that there is an increasing disconnect between functions. Although leadership support of CX is there, ownership is not.

The Strategic Imperative

Before delving into the details of designing an efficient form of governance for CX within organizations, and as it is essential to bridge the gap between strategy and execution, it is important to look first at the role of CX practitioners when it comes to developing the customer experience strategy.

As CX practitioners, we often fall into the trap of developing a strategy that is just too 'outside-in' without effective consideration of the overall corporate strategic objectives. This ultimately hinders the success of implementing the CX strategy. I have noticed that the common top of mind answers stated by CX professionals when asked about the objectives of their CX strategies are to increase customer satisfaction and/ or reduce customer effort. It is rarely the case that the strategic benefits of improving satisfaction or reducing effort are directly highlighted. It actually takes a couple of iterations and a few hints towards corporate objectives to make CX professionals arrive at an answer that is more global to the organization, where revenues, bottom lines, cost optimization and other overarching strategic objectives become intact.

As we preach empathy more often than not, we CX professionals need to practice what we preach but internally this time. We need to empathize with our C-Suite and other functional players within the organization to ensure alignment on the corporate strategic objectives so we can increase the chances of success for our CX strategy and the related initiatives.

Building CX Cadence

After securing alignment on the CX strategy, focusing the efforts on implementation needs to come next. Having an enabled core CX team that covers all mandates of the CX practice is not enough. More enablement is needed by engaging key players in the organization and putting the right governance into action.

By definition, governance is a system by which a structure and processes for decision making and accountability are designed to influence how an organization sets and achieves objectives, and how it optimizes performance.[2]

In corporate environments, governance is usually part of an operating model that details how the operations of a specific function or the whole organization work. It aims at building a certain tempo for how to achieve certain objectives. When it comes to CX, governance is often tackled in the form of cross-functional committees, which I like to refer to as Centers of Excellence (CoE).

Essentially, defining the scope of the CoE is a key step to ensure the foundations are set right. Figure 2 below illustrates the main elements of the scope, which are:

- The objective: Why do we have the CoE?
- Strategic pillars or streams: What will it focus on?
- Enablers: What and who will be utilized to achieve success?
- Main indicators: How will success look like?

Figure 2 – Customer Experience Center of Excellence
© 2021 Mohamad El-Hinnawi

Beyond defining the scope, the success of the transformation relies on how the governance is applied across the organization while securing the following key factors:

1. Top Management Mandate And Full Support

To ensure participation and inspiration of the selected members in the CoE, a clear mandate should be set by top management. It is only then when CX organizational gaps will be overcome. Middle management and CoE members will only support the overall efforts of customer centric transformation and be inspired by them if there is a clear mandate and full support by senior management. This also needs to be reflected in the performance measures that those members are evaluated against.

2. Establishment Of A Design Authority

A design authority needs to be identified within the CoE. The main role of this authority is to ensure that results adhere to the original design. As one of the main mandates of the CoE is to design and co-create customer journeys, the recommendations and initiatives that result out of the journeys need to be executed as per the anticipated experience design guidelines. If we look back at the daily calls from my eCommerce company, we can tell that there was no design authority governing the anticipated improvement. On the contrary, it seems that the idea of confirming the address before delivery came up so the field team does not struggle in the operations; however, there was no one confirming that the idea fits the experience guidelines.

3. Accountability Of The Work

One of the main objectives of the CoE is making sure that there is a common target that the whole organization is aligned on and is working together towards achieving it. To put it in the CX context, as Customer Satisfaction (CSAT) is one of the main indicators that all of us CX professionals look at, it would be essential to make CSAT a shared target for the whole organization. As we define the scope of the CoE, we will define the main attributes or pillars that will be managed within it. Assuming that there is a specific stream for products, there would be a specific CSAT for products which will be cascaded to each one of the stakeholders engaged in the 'products' stream, and will have its own weight on their score cards.

4. Engagement Of The Whole Organization

Success will only be achieved if the whole organization is engaged and aligned on the efforts. Instead of having only functional owners tackle initiatives related to the relevant stream, all champions from across the organization will be involved. Think of the value driven by having a salesperson engaged in improving initiatives related to communication. This is an opportunity to have a positive impact on the way sales is done and avoid things like wrong information about the value of the product and overpromising. Similarly, a marketeer who is engaged in the 'channels' stream initiatives, will have a better understanding of the different channels and eventually improve the product to facilitate its sales through a specific channel.

5. Communication Of Results

Having a CoE increases the chance of success while implementing the CX related initiatives. Communicating results and celebrating success are very important for positive reinforcement. It is essential to share the results to motivate the CoE members, align other stakeholders in the organization, and set the model for success.

In addition to the aforementioned success factors, and similar to any other function, a CoE requires its own operating model. Aside from its structure, roles of its champions, methodology and how often it meets, the most important thing is to look at the results that are being generated. A CoE is usually in place to standardize operations, prioritize work, avoid restructuring and have cross-functional alignment. It is not the entire organization that needs to change, but the way the organization coordinates its CX efforts and collaboration across functions[3].

Failure of planting the right seed to maximize the benefits of a CX Center of Excellence will defeat the purpose of its existence.

To keep in mind, the scale of the organization heavily impacts the kind of governance that needs to be put in place. We should also consider the external parties and vendors that contribute to our value chain. While writing this piece, I came to know that the eCommerce company has its address confirmation calls outsourced to a third party.

Can you think of how important governance is in such context?

References

1. NTT (2020). 2020 Global Customer Experience Benchmarking Report. NTT Ltd.

2. Governance Today (2020). Governance: What is it and why is it important? www.governancetoday.com

3. Harting, A., Hauptmann, M., Steinpichler, C., Freesemann, M., Rudolph, M., Lux, T. (2019). *How the right CX Operating Model can pave the way to future success*. Deloitte Digital

About Mohamad El-Hinnawi, CCXP

Mohamad El-Hinnawi, CCXP is a Partner at New Metrics, an experience management consultancy, where he leads the Experience Management and Digital consulting practice.

Mohamad has more than 16 years of experience in CX and digital transformation strategies, VoC design, customer journey mapping, and channel optimization, with employment and consulting engagements in more than 10 countries and for clients in multiple industries.

He is a Recognized Training Provider (RTP) for the Certified Customer Experience Professional (CCXP), and was featured in CXPA's "Who's Who of Customer Experience" as a top customer experience professional with advanced maturity and broad strategic knowledge in the discipline. He is also a member of the Board of Directors at the Customer Institute.

Mohamad is a regular Keynote Speaker on CX and Digital Transformation in regional and international conferences and has judged and chaired at several leading CX awards events. He has published many articles on designated platforms like the CXPA Blog, Customer Think, and CXM.world.

Contacts and Links

LinkedIn: *https://www.linkedin.com/in/mohamadhinnawi*

Twitter: *https://www.twitter.com/mdhinnawi*

CX And Quality Management - Evolution Or Integration And Who Should Be In Charge?

Marc Karschies CCXP, CXPA RTP

Judging by the number of Digital and CX transformation projects, books, blogs, and awards popping up all over social media and conference agendas, Customer Experience appears to be all the rave right now. Traditional KPI and Product Development frameworks are upended to make way for new measures along Net Promoter Scores (NPS), and Agile and Design Thinking methodologies. New fancy job titles and projects seem to indicate that even those areas in the organization not traditionally involved with customers want to be involved in CX and EX and get in on the limelight.

But what happened to good old-fashioned Quality Management? Is it now antiquated or even obsolete? And does it make sense to move responsibilities and budgets away from those QA, QC and general Quality Management functions?

The short answer is: No. For sure there are overlapping areas of responsibility, and the detailed answer might be more complicated based on the organizational structures and maturity of the organization. However, Quality Management and Customer Experience Management serve different objectives, both necessary to ensure high levels of Customer Satisfaction, and enabling the organization to generate value for both the organization and the customer.

Definitions of Customer Experience Management And Quality Management

While this article will later explore approaches to roles and responsibilities of Quality and CX managers in organizations, it is important to clear the air on what we actually mean by CX and Quality.

The Customer Experience Professionals Association (CXPA) defines Customer Experience (CX) as

"the perception that customers have of an organization - one that is formed based on interactions across all touchpoints, people, and technology over time."

Many quality definitions by pioneers (Gurus) of quality management (aka 'way back then') also see quality through the eyes of the customer, e.g. Juran's 'Fitness for Use', or Feigenbaum's 'Quality is what the user, the customer, says it is.'

So, thinking on behalf of the customer is not new, and both, CX and Quality, could claim they should be the ones working on aligning the organization towards more customer centricity. The differences come in regard to HOW an organization should best approach the management of resources towards a (strategically) targeted experience by customers. CXPA defines CX Management as

"the set of practices that an organization employs to meet (or exceed) customers' expectations"

This unfortunately leaves this question quite open for interpretation, exemplifying why there are so many competing, and often opposing, approaches to CX Management currently in the market, ranging from focus on Digitization and "Segments of One" to Employee Centricity and Cultural Transformation.

Quality Gurus (with the added advantage of tried and trusted implementations over time) tended to be more precise in how to approach achievement of quality. E.g. Deming's "Good quality means a predictable degree of uniformity and dependability with a quality standard suited to the customer" or Crosby's "conformance to requirements" are often cited by quality managers as the way to go. Even the American Society for Quality defines Quality along more technical interpretations as:

"In technical usage, quality can have two meanings:

1. the characteristics of a product or service that bear on its ability to satisfy stated or implied needs;

2. a product or service free of deficiencies."

Juran and Feigenbaum (both significant Quality Gurus) on the other hand took a more holistic 'Total' approach to Quality management, meaning that their Total Quality Management (TQM) and Total Quality Control (TQC) approaches were very much aligned with modern CX approaches all along, and arguably could question the hype of CX as they have been around (yet often forgotten) for several decades.

Hence, should Quality Management be discarded and make way for CX? Absolutely not. In effect CX is merely an evolutionary step of a variety of Quality Management philosophies and as such QM provides a wealth of established and still applicable tools and techniques that can be used to manage the organization towards the target experience.

QM And CX Toolsets Available To Manage Specific Scenarios And Problems

Yet, if CX and Quality Management are so closely related, why is there so much competition between Quality Managers and CX Managers? Simply said, there is a lot of pride, praise and budget involved that lets many managers vie for attention within the newly re-discovered excitement of Senior Management for the customer.

When QM and CX approaches and philosophies were designed, they had a specific scenario or problem set in mind, and as such tend to be better in solving certain problems and scenarios, but not others. Like a hammer is a great tool to break down a wall or to affix a nail, it is not the best tool to use when trying to turn a screw. Screwdrivers are arguably not best in removing a nail, but can do a great job in doing so on a screw. You could use the screwdriver's handle or a wrench to hit in a nail, even though it is likely less efficient or effective than a hammer. Thus, many of the tools were designed for a specific purpose but have multipurpose capabilities that skilled professionals can utilize.

Likewise, Quality Management and CX toolsets excel in some scenarios, but not in others (or can even be harmful if applied incorrectly or excessively). They can also overlap as multitool sets with similar tools but different naming as they all borrow heavily from each other.

While the following will likely trigger strong responses from respective QM practitioners (especially those that identify themselves as experts in only one of the toolsets without fully understanding or appreciating the capabilities of the others), it helps in taking a couple of steps back and reviewing the toolset landscape more objectively (I am aware that I grossly simplify the following descriptions, but it helps to make the points).

- Six Sigma had been designed to provide toolsets on statistical process control and subsequent improvements and process consistency, but is hardly the most customer centric methodology to trigger target emotional responses in customers (as in Customer Experiences).
- Lean (and its root, the Toyota Production System or TPS) was designed to remove waste from processes and organizations in general, but not to establish a strong customer centric mindset or culture.
- TQM was designed as a people centric approach to integrate the whole organization into a customer centric culture mindset, yet it lacks the detailed tools to manage processes or technology due to its focus on people.

- Digital Transformation is great to improve channel choice and utilization. However, not all customers are ready yet to part with talking to real humans and seal a deal with a firm handshake (albeit the global pandemic has changed many traditional approaches in this space).

The point here is that depending on the Corporate Strategy, the type of targeted customers and their respective needs and expectations, the gaps and bottlenecks within the organization that stand in the way of achieving the organizational objectives, and the maturity of the organization and the employees within, will determine which methodology and toolset is best for that specific scenario. If customers are upset because the organization constantly fails to deliver consistent processes and services, improving process consistency through Six Sigma tools might be the best approach to influence the CX. If the expectation of the customer is impacted due to value perception (price is too high in comparison to the benefits provided), Lean could help in removing wasteful and time-consuming activities and thus improve the perceived cost, efficiency and value experience. If employees are not engaged and provide grumpy service to internal and external customers, TQM culture change programs can help to improve the service mentality across the whole organization, aligning internal as well as customer facing areas towards a common CX goal.

In any of these scenarios, "traditional" Quality Management toolsets are likely the better choice to manage the organizational outcomes that influence customer experience, rather than pure digitization or branding and marketing activities which seem to be the foremost publicised CX initiatives and strategies of many organizations.

Maturity And Strategy Of The Organization Should Drive Toolset Choice

As outlined above, there are a wide range of toolsets to choose from and application scenarios encountered within an organization. Identifying the QM and CX maturity of an organization along five main stages can help decide which ones to use.

"Start-up" is a phase where the organization is identifying itself in the early stages of organizational development. Often only few customers have been acquired yet, and many tales of such companies can be found on Social Media telling of their absolute customer centricity where e.g. founders and CEOs answer personally to each and every complaint or customer experience mishap. In such environments with few customers and employees, a strong sense of corporate culture and belonging and decentralized decision making and empowerment, most employees tend to be customer centric and go above and beyond the needed to ensure highest levels of customer satisfaction.

However, while in this stage there is certainly an economic requirement to satisfy and retain all possible customers (as any customer leaving could lead to disastrous financial outcomes to cash flow and company survival), there is also a flipside to this style. In most organizations such an approach is not sustainable once the organization starts to scale up. Additional layers and specialized employees are added to cope with the increased business, thus often watering down the initial culture and customer engagement.

"Scaling Up" therefore requires organizations to become more consistent in their approaches and processes, so to ensure additional staff and customers can effectively and efficiently be onboarded and integrated into the organizational environment. Focus on processes and consistent structures, documentation and auditing of adherence to the standards become more prevalent, in turn reducing the prospects of ad-hoc exceptions to resolve customer issues in a flexible and "high experience" manner. QM toolsets like Six Sigma or ISO certifications are often used to improve consistency levels, and structure the organization into a process driven way. While this is to some extent a necessity to cope with the scaling requirements of the organization, arguably customer experience suffers, especially if customer expectations and branding still recall or remind of the high levels of individualized CX during the Start-Up phase.

'Improving Business Model and Profitability' are vital for the long-term success of organizations, as waste and inefficiencies built up during previous scaling or adjustment phases. Not removing such waste will inadvertently impact the profitability and viability of many businesses, thus making it harder to provide a strong value proposition as either less benefits can be provided to customers, less funding will be available for innovation and business improvements, or too high a cost is charged to the clients to cover the financial requirements of the organization. Lean toolsets (often combined with Six Sigma approaches to ensure consistency is maintained) are frequently used to achieve such waste reduction and efficiency gains.

"Clear Corporate Identity and Branding" become the focus of organizations that have been able to scale up and retain/ achieve efficiencies and profitability, and now want to go back to or revive the roots and customer centricity culture of the early start-up environment. Focus often shifts to holistic culture and people centric approaches. Toolsets used in people centric environments often include those from Total Quality Management (TQM) and incorporate alignment with strategic management systems and Balanced Scorecard approaches.

"Strategic Customer Centricity" represents the highest level of maturity when organizations have been able to grow through, and retained the gains of, the previous stages. If the organization managed to do so, it

- will have a strong customer centric storyline and history (from Start-Up),

- achieved a track record of reliability and consistency of their processes and service delivery,
- will be profitable and efficient to ensure the business will continue to be around in the future, and
- have been able to align the whole organization around a robust corporate culture and people centric approach.

At this stage, an organization can confidently promise and deliver a value proposition to customers, where the customer can rely on not being disappointed. This will drive positive experiences as defined by CXPA: "the perception that customers have of an organization - one that is formed based on interactions across all touchpoints, people, and technology over time".

So, Who Should Be In Charge, QM Or CX?

The above should provide sufficient context to make the answer clear by now. Depending on the maturity of the organization and the predominant outstanding gaps in delivering to the customer as promised, focus (and control) should be given to the relevant QM or CX specialists to solve those underlying gaps as necessary.

Once they are solved, the control should be passed on to the next stage experts as no CX nor QM manager will ever be an absolute master across all methodologies and approaches. While hard to swallow for some, QM and CX managers should openly acknowledge where their own knowledge and expertise gaps exist, and seek out and hand over the reins to the respective experts needed for the organization to achieve the next maturity stage. The higher the maturity, the more strategic and holistic the roles and responsibilities will become, but relevant expertise and continuous management of the other QM areas should still be performed.

Most organizations fail in achieving true excellence in CX due to trying to prematurely jump to the next (or even final) maturity stage without having properly and sustainably implemented the underlying qualities (consistency, efficiency, culture). They try to go after short term wins, tactical projects, awards and brand recognition. This might cause customers to be delighted in the short term (or at least have their expectations set at high levels), but will leave them thoroughly disappointed once the fake façade of CX and customer centricity crumbles without the proper quality foundation.

So only organizations that have managed to accomplish (and maintain) all maturity stages and organize CX in a holistic strategic manner throughout the organization will be recognized for their excellence in CX.

About Marc Karschies CCXP, CXPA RTP

Marc Karschies, Managing Partner at KCA Consultants, is considered one of the leading experts on Corporate & Customer Experience Strategy and Integrated Service Quality Management in the MENA region. On top of his international consultancy work, he is a frequent expert speaker and award judge on CX and Service Quality Management & Strategy. He is an active member of CXPA as one of the Community Leaders of CXPA UAE, holds the CCXP certification, and is an accredited Recognized Training Provider (RTP) of CXPA.

Before starting KCA's boutique CX consultancy and training business in 2013, Marc built a strong practitioner background with over 20 years in various senior management positions in Financial Services (e.g. Operations Director/VP at Diners Club Europe and Citibank International, and Head of Group Service Quality at Emirates NBD Banking Group).

He held various master level teaching assignments at HULT International Business School and Middlesex University and served in Senior Assessor and Team leader positions in the Dubai Quality Award and Dubai Human Development Award.

Originally from Germany, Marc holds an Executive MBA from London Business School, a BBA in Finance and Banking (HfB Frankfurt), and a wide range of professional certifications, incl. Certified Customer Experience Professional (CCXP), ASQ Certified Quality Manager (CMQ/OE), Six Sigma Black Belt, and is a Kaplan-Norton Balanced Scorecard Certified Graduate. In 2018, Marc has been awarded the 'Quality Professional of the Year' Award by the American Society for Quality, reflecting the high appreciation of his work within the profession.

Contacts And Links

www.kca-consultants.com

https://ae.linkedin.com/in/marckarschies

Twitter: KCA_Consultants

Empathy Is NOT Enough

Sandra D P Thompson

While the practice of empathy has certainly helped organisations achieve greater employee engagement and better business performance[1], it's not enough to create thriving emotional connections between staff and customers and between colleagues. We need thriving emotional connections because they lead to profitable loyalty[2].

Empathy certainly encourages people to listen more and it is true that we often feel better understood when someone is empathetic towards us. The act of empathising could however be fundamentally flawed[3] and according to insight brought to us by neuroscientists, it's impossible for us to empathise in a meaningful way.

In this chapter, I intend to challenge your view of empathy and ask you to consider its limitations. I will invite you to explore the skill of Emotional Intelligence (EI) and the positive impact it could have on you and your business. I will explain how the 12 competencies[4] which comprise the skill of EI give us the opportunity to become resilient, resourceful, balanced and successful individuals.

Finally, you will learn how the skill of EI brings individuals and businesses better health and greater happiness[5], increased profitability[6] along with stronger and authentic emotional connections.

The Rising Popularity Of Empathy

It seems to me that the term empathy has been increasingly used in recent years. There are an increasing number of articles about businesses becoming empathetic with staff. I've experienced a warmer tone in brand communications. I've noted further discussion about empathy training in contact centres and read more about leaders needing to become more empathetic.

I believe that the effects of the global pandemic have changed the way people perceive relationships and the emotions associated with them. The global fight against the virus has changed people's perspective. I don't think that customers or colleagues have changed per se, but I think that their expectations, their values and beliefs have become more pronounced. They expect deeper understanding, kindness and thoughtfulness. These needs could be met through EI, which incorporates empathy, rather than through empathy alone.

What Is Empathy?

Let's take a moment now to explore what empathy is.

There are three levels of empathy. The highest level is cognitive empathy. We think we can relate to the other person because we think we know how they are feeling.

The second level is deeper. This is emotional empathy. In this case, we perceive that we are actually feeling a similar emotion to the person we are attempting to empathise with.

The third and final level is compassionate empathy. In this case, the individual empathising is so moved by the feelings they have in response to the other person's behaviour, that they are moved to act. This is the ideal level for customer experiences because employees want to help, they feel good when they can take the action the customer expects. Customers also want brands to evidence their empathy. They don't want a brand to just say they empathise, they want them to take the appropriate action to demonstrate their understanding and caring.

Now I should like to challenge your view of empathy. We'll start with an explanation of emotions from growing evidence in neuroscience and move onto the idea of rational compassion.

What Are Emotions?

Neuroscientist Lisa Feldman Barrett[7] and her team have spent years looking at images of the brain from MRi scans. They have pored over thousands of reports about the function of the brain. They now challenge widely held beliefs about how emotions are made.

According to Feldman Barrett, emotions are a prediction of something that is about to happen. We feel a sensation before we attach a meaning to it. These meanings are influenced by three things:

1. Our socialisation – our thinking is influenced by the values and beliefs of our parents, teachers and other authoritative figures when we were growing up.
2. Our experience – experiences create emotions and we attach meaning to them. The meaning can be positive, neutral or less positive. This means that experiences or the anticipation of an experience could generate positive, neutral or less positive emotions depending on the meaning we attached to the emotions generated when the experience happened.
3. Our context – emotions are understood in context. Feldman Barrett demonstrates this point beautifully when she shows an image of Serena William's face at a tennis tournament. Looking at the close up we perceive the tennis champion as upset. When Feldman Barrett zooms out and shows the whole image, we see Serena Williams holding a Wimbledon trophy and we realise that she has been moved to tears of joy in her triumph[8].

Emotions are therefore as unique as fingerprints and our expression of emotions are unique too because everyone has attributed different meanings to the sensations they feel due to the points above.

When we empathise, we think that we know how someone is feeling because we believe that we think or feel in the same way. In most cases we can't truly create a meaningful connection to someone empathetically on a cognitive, emotional or compassionate way because the emotions we are thinking about or experiencing are our own. Our emotions have been shaped by our own socialisation, experiences and our interpretation of the context of the situation. Most of us don't even realise that we are responding to our own emotions when we are trying to empathise.

To empathise in a meaningful way, you require the skill of EI which affords you a high degree of self-awareness and self-management. These competencies make you adept at understanding and recognising your own emotions and they equip you with techniques to better recognise and understand emotions in others. This means that when you attempt to empathise with EI you are more likely to recognise your own emotions and you'll be able to see and hear the emotions of others more clearly.

A Case For Rational Compassion?

Psychologist Paul Bloom explains that we make ineffective and sometimes unethical decisions when we are guided by empathy. This could mean that the act of empathy is fundamentally flawed. When we observe something and we attempt to empathise, we are heavily influenced by our unconscious biases and prejudices and so we don't see things clearly.

Bloom claims that when we empathise, we are more likely to have a positive view of people 'like us' and look unfavourably on those who are less 'like us'. By choosing rational compassion rather than empathy, the person being 'compassionate' cares about the person exhibiting emotions and invites them to discuss how they are feeling without trying to empathise at all. The person receiving the compassion feels heard and valued. Bloom states that this approach is more helpful as we are not attaching meaning, interpretation or influencing what they say and feel.

Having defined empathy, explored emotion and rational compassion, it's time to talk about EI and explore what it has to offer Customer Experience Management (CX) and how the adoption of the skill will deliver more sustainable results than empathy alone.

Emotional Intelligence – Creating Thriving Emotional Connections

The term EI was popularised by Daniel Goleman and his 1995 book, Emotional Intelligence, why EQ matters more than IQ[9]. His EI definition is:

> *"Emotional Intelligence is your ability to recognise and understand emotions in yourself and others. It's your ability to manage your behaviour and relationships[10]."*

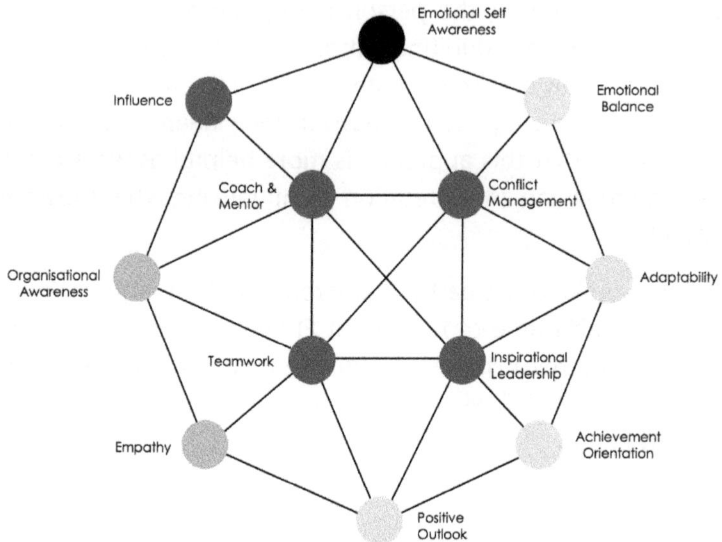

Figure 1: Empathy is one of the 12 competencies of Emotional Intelligence Adapted from Goleman, D. Boyatzis, R., Emotional Intelligence Has 12 Elements. Which do you need to work in? Massachusetts, Harvard Business Review, 2017.

I've compiled a list of the 12 competencies comprising EI and described the difference they could make to individuals in customer influencing roles. People like you. I should like to invite you to consider how the collective adoption of all competencies could result in profitable loyalty from colleagues and customers in your businesses.

1. **Self-awareness** – understanding your own emotions and the way they effect performance is hugely valuable in any CX role. Knowing your strengths and limitations makes you decisive and gives you the self-confidence to continue creating the change customers value.

2. **Emotional balance** – self-regulation is an important quality not only for your health but also for the growth of your relationships. CX roles face challenges and this competency helps you maintain your effectiveness even when things get stressful.

3. **Adaptability** – flexibility means you can handle change and you are resourceful. Encouraging others to pivot, CX roles juggle demands from across the business, evolve and generate fresh ideas or innovative approaches.

4. **Achievement orientation** – meeting or exceeding a standard of excellence. That's you. When you have this competency you are continuously improving, you set challenging goals, take calculated risks and achieve greater success.

5. **Positive Outlook** – resilience is strongly correlated to positive outlook[11]. We know you have a tough job and with a positive outlook you are more likely to see opportunities and remain persistent in pursing business aims, despite setbacks and obstacles.

6. **Empathy** – building on what has been said already, you have the ability to sense others' feelings and how they see things. You can also sense unspoken emotions as you actively listen to understand the other person's point of view. This is a very different type of empathy compared to the one described earlier. This empathy is applied after you have gained self-awareness and the ability to manage your emotions. This means that when you empathise with these competencies you are more likely to recognise your biases and prejudices and you can separate your emotions from those belonging to the person you are attempting to empathise with. This is a meaningful approach.

7. **Organisational awareness** – critical for influencing and persuading people across your organisation. It allows you to read the 'vibe' [emotional energy and power relationships] of a group. You are able to correctly identify the influencers, networks, and dynamics within the organisation.

8. **Influence** – CX roles must express their ideas in a way that will appeal to others. With this competency you gather support with relative ease and you lead and engage groups who are mobilised and ready to do what's necessary to give customers what they value.

9. **Coach and mentor** – Individuals get more out of coaches than managers[12]. This approach enables you to help others thrive through the development of their self-awareness and accountability.

10. **Conflict Management** – having the ability to support others through emotional or tense situations. You help others resolve disagreements and define solutions. In most cases you manage to avoid conflict using competencies listed earlier.

11. **Teamwork** – building an environment of respect, helpfulness and cooperation, you work effectively with others contributing to a team spirit, building positive emotional connections and enhancing the identity of the team. You achieve more together.

12. **Inspirational leadership** – you can motivate and guide people to get the right job done for colleagues and for customers. This approach brings out the best in you and others.

Invest In EI, Not Just Empathy

Customer experience management needs the skill of EI, not just empathy on its own.

When we use empathy on its own we are limited in our ability to make authentic, meaningful and sustainable emotional connections. When we apply the competency of empathy within the skill of EI we are more likely to create emotional connections that lead to profitable loyalty. We also gain so many additional competencies. These are the competencies CX roles need to be even more effective.

EI isn't just an optional soft skill, it delivers some impressive hard results. Here are just a few of the outcomes achieved through the adoption of EI [more stats are available]:

- Research has shown that sales managers for the world's largest cosmetics company with the skill of emotional intelligence sold almost $100,000 more a year than their colleagues who lack these competencies[13].

- Businesses in the legal sector have been able to charge at least 8% more per hour, per partner when they exercise this skill with clients and colleagues[14].
- Individuals with the skill of EI lead happier and healthier lives.[15]

The skill of emotional intelligence offers individuals and businesses incredible opportunities; not only health and wellbeing benefits but financial rewards. It seems that little is known about EI within customer experience management, people opt for empathy and so its potential has not yet been recognised.

It is hoped that giving EI more exposure, greater explanation and providing evidence of its positive impact more customer experience roles will consider investing in EI [and the empathy within it] rather than empathy alone.

The skill of EI brings resilience, balance, resourcefulness and success to CX roles. They will increasingly need these qualities as the perspectives of employees and customers continue to change in these uncertain times. It's time to check EI out.

References

1. Joshua Feast interviewed by Adrian Swinscoe on a Punk CX podcast. E205.

2. Hill-Wilson, M., *Emotive CX for Customer interaction,* New voice media, 2018.

3. Bloom, P., *Against Empathy. The Case for Rational Compassion.* London, The Bodley Head, 2016.

4. Goleman, D. Boyatzis, R., *Emotional Intelligence Has 12 Elements. Which do you need to work in?* Massachusetts, Harvard Business Review, 2017.

5. Goleman, D. *Social Intelligence. The new science of human relationships.* London, Arrow, 2007.

6. Bradberry, T. Greaves, J., *Emotional Intelligence 2.0.* Michigan, Brilliance Audio, 2009.

7. Feldman Barrett, L., *How emotions are made. The secret life of the brain*, London, Pan Macmillan, 2017.

8. Feldman Barrett, L., You aren't at the mercy of your emotions – your brain creates them. TED@IBM, 2017.

9. Goleman, D., *Emotional Intelligence, Why EQ matters more than IQ.* London, Bloomsbury Publishing plc, 1995.

10. Goleman, D., *Emotional Intelligence, Why EQ matters more than IQ.* London, Bloomsbury Publishing plc, 1995.

11. Seligman, M., *Post Traumatic Growth and Building Resilience.* Massachusetts, Harvard Business Review, 2018.

12. Ibarra, H. Scoular, A., *The Leader as Coach.* Massachusetts, Harvard Business Review, 2019.

13. Spencer & Spencer, 1993

14. Muir, R., *Beyond Smart: Lawyering with Emotional Intelligence.* Chicago, American Bar Association, 2018.

15. Hasson, J., *Emotional Intelligence: Managing emotions to make a positive on your life and career.* Chichester, Wiley, 2014

About Sandra D P Thompson

Sandra Thompson is the founding director of The Ei Evolution, a consultancy that provides organisations with bespoke support which improves their employee and customer experiences. Sandra achieves this through coaching, consulting, training and post graduate courses which help individuals and teams adopt the skill of Emotional Intelligence and apply it to their business practices. Sandra's clients have included: Arsenal Football Club, Waitrose, Vodafone, Open University and Network Rail.

Sandra is a part time lecturer at Pearson College London on the topics of People Management and Leadership and Professional Behaviours & Customer Management. She is a Fellow of the Chartered Institute of Marketing [FCIM] and in May 2020 she became the first Goleman Emotional Intelligence Coach in the UK having been taught by Dr. Goleman and his faculty. Sandra gave her first TEDx in October 2020 on Ei, CX and remote work and was voted 17th in the world ranking of CX Stars in 2021.

Contacts And Links

www.eievolution.com

Sandra@eievolution.com

https://www.linkedin.com/in/cxeisandra/

3. VoC Insights And Understandings

Analyse and understand your customer to drive change

Experience Your Customers' Experiences! Please!

Bob Azman

The only way to truly understand your customers' experiences is to experience them yourself.

In 1992, I read a Harvard Business Review (HBR) article entitled, *Staple Yourself to An Order* by Shapiro, Rangan and Sviokla. It was later re-published as an HBR Classic in 2004. For me, it was the beginning of a transformation that would positively and continually impact my perspective on creating and executing effective customer experience strategy for nearly thirty years. The authors define the order management cycle as *"the process you use to forecast sales, generate orders, establish prices, receive and prioritize orders, schedule production, provide the product or service ordered, bill the customer, and handle returns and post-sales service."* Their definition is today's description of an end-to-end customer journey with your products and services. I strongly encourage you to read it as a complement to this chapter.

For a moment, let's set aside the journey maps. Shelve the surveys. Defer buying new technologies that promise to solve your problems. Pause spending your valuable time and energy trying to get executive buy-in. Instead, consider an approach that is much simpler and even more telling. Understand what your customers' experiences are when buying your products and services.

Let me explain this concept (the why). Below is a sampling of recent contacts with a broad range of companies across a wide variety of industries (consumer goods; automobiles; business services; big box retailers; online marketers; financial services, etc.). Have you experienced any of these situations? I have.

- Mobile applications that have constant chat windows that impede your ability to complete an order.
- Websites that insist on pop-ups on a variety of subjects every time I switched to a different product view or page.
- Functions on a website that are simply broken. *Page Not Found 404 Error.*
- Chat Bots that are useless in answering questions and good at wasting time when a live agent could address it in less time.
- Agents who weren't properly trained on company procedures or practices and had to *ask a supervisor* who wasn't available.
- Templated emails that don't answer my question or use company jargon to convey a solution.
- Two or more layers of "press one" interactive voice response units each with nine options.
- Constant promotion of a product while simultaneously receiving a notice that my order is delayed due to higher-than-expected orders of that same product.
- Hold messages that repeatedly say, *Due to higher than planned call volumes, we are experiencing longer hold times than normal.*
- Automated messages that assure me if I answer all their questions up front, I won't have to repeat it to an agent. False!

I have more examples and my guess is so do you. I figured you would lose interest or get as frustrated as I have been if you read too many more. None of these are made up. These are real experiences that happened to me recently and repeatedly.

Why do these things keep happening? They keep happening because the people making decisions in your organization are not buying their own products or navigating their own websites or trying to muddle through endless interactive voice response units. Trust me. If they encountered their customers' experiences, action would be taken on the prior mentioned bad experiences.

Why don't marketing and sales professionals, product managers, operations managers, and customer service leaders as well as those in human resources, accounting, and IT, experience their own experience? In fact, why isn't everyone from the CEO on down participating in this exercise? As the HBR article states (albeit a bit outdated), *A typical CEO woos clients on the golf course or at meetings devoted to high-level questions. Here's a better idea: Recreate the client's experience by following an order through your plant.* It matters not whether you are in a business-to-business or business-to-consumer organization. You can do this same exercise regardless of the product or service you sell. Several years ago, I was speaking on this topic and a person in the back of the room raised his hand and said, "I work for a large construction equipment manufacturer, what do you want me to do, build a bulldozer just to experience my customer's experience?" I will let you guess what my answer was to his question.

Everyone must experience your customers' (or members, patients, clients, guests) experiences. Please!

To pursue this nearly thirty-year old idea that frankly is more breakthrough and innovative than the many ideas available today, here's a roadmap to execute the concept (the what). First things first. You need to establish a CX foundation to align your actions and engage the organization.

- Write down what your organization's customer experience is today. Next, write down what you want in your organization's customer experience. A CX strategy needs to be clearly defined, easy to understand, aspirational, specific, and measurable.

- Share your strategy, even if it is not perfect, with employees across all functions of your organization. Seek their input and feedback. The employees closest to the customers are a wealth of knowledge. They clearly hear what your organization does and does not do well.

- Does each department and each member of that department understand the role they play in delivering a better customer experience?

- Brainstorm in advance what you want employees to look for as they experience your customers' experiences. A few suggested questions to consider are:

- Is the sales team knowledgeable about your products?

- Are the promotions from marketing clear and concise? Easily obtained and executed?

- Does your website and mobile application make it easy to do business with you?

- Do you provide inventory status of your products while ordering?

- Is your shipping process easy to understand?

- Is your customer service team trained to answer questions about products or services? Do they have the authority to make decisions on the spot?

- Are your invoices, billing, and credit card options up to date so customers have a secure choice in how they pay you?

- What guarantees do you have? Are they unconditional, clearly stated, and easy for customers to invoke?

- Is your return process simple for the customer to follow?

Now that you have the why and the what in place, it's time to execute the strategy (the how):

- Seek an employee volunteer from each department and with varying levels of authority so you have a good cross section of both frontline staff and managers participating in the process.
- Develop a system so they can buy from your websites and mobile applications and provide feedback on their experiences. No need to hire mystery shoppers or engage research firms to conduct this exercise.
- If it is not feasible to physically make the purchase due to product or service limitations, then grab a live customer order and follow it through your system from beginning to end. Better yet, engage with your customer and have them walk the order through the process with you!

  - Yes, it can be scary and even risky to engage with your customers in this process, but it doesn't have to be. Explaining the purpose and outcomes to your customers will reduce the risk and provide you valuable firsthand learning from them.
  - This is not a one-time exercise but an ongoing event that requires a single point of contact to manage the process and report the results.

- Create a closed-loop system. A process that gathers the feedback and analyzes it for common issues, then provides the results to the appropriate department and lastly holds them accountable for fixing the problem and creating a better experience.

  - Celebrate the improvement with employees and customers for a moment and then move on to the next opportunity for a better experience.

- Besides these steps in the process, I also encourage you to monitor your technology daily. It can malfunction.

Upgrades can sometimes fail. Bugs happen. Make sure you are the first to know about it and not your customers.

- Is your interactive voice response unit working properly and routing customers to the proper department?
- Are your other supportive technologies providing the right information at the right time to those in your organization that need it?

As noted in the HBR article, stapling yourself to an order can improve customer satisfaction, eliminate silos, and improve financial performance. It is however, but one component of an effective voice of customer (VOC) process within your organization. If you don't have one, this approach is a great way to start. If you do have a VOC process in place this can complement efforts already underway. The purpose of any VOC process is to paint a picture of what customers are saying about your products and services. It is one of the six core competencies identified by the Customer Experience Professional Association (CXPA.org) as integral to the successful execution of an experience management strategy in your organization.

There is much talk about engaging employees and customers' experiences as mutual stakeholders in reaching a beneficial outcome. Once this concept is embedded in the DNA of the organization, it will become "the way we do business" with your customers. Customers have a long memory. They remember the companies that invested in the experience despite limited resources. They reward those organizations with loyalty and positive word-of-mouth that will last a lot longer than you might imagine.

For employees, this approach lets them learn about functions within their organization that they may never have experienced or understood in the past. It provides them with a better understanding of the organization's approach to customer experience with a greater impact than a poster on a conference room wall or quarterly newsletter. By seeing the steps in the order fulfillment process firsthand, they gain a better perspective and appreciation for the roles and responsibilities of their fellow employees. It goes without saying that better employee engagement means better customer experiences.

I often read about and hear from organizations that are frustrated when they see less than a 5-star online review. But when I discover they've failed to address many of the items I've listed above, clearly, they deserved the substandard rating.

Consumers have had to adjust and transform many of their traditional ways of doing business during this extraordinary pandemic. Many of the organizations we buy from need to do the same thing.

First impressions make a difference! Do you know what your customer's first impression is of your organization? If not, maybe it's time to experience what they experience when working with you! Please!

About Bob Azman

Bob Azman is Founder and CEO of Innovative CX Solutions, LLC a Customer Experience Consulting Firm specializing in CX Design and Execution, Sales and Service Experience Design, Customer Service, Supply Chain and Operations Management and Talent Development. He is a Past Chairman of the Board of the Customer Experience Professional Association (CXPA.org). He is a Certified Customer Experience Professional.

Bob has a wealth of diverse, global operations and leadership experiences as an executive at organizations such as Carlson Wagonlit Travel, Thomson Reuters, Ceridian, and Deluxe Corporation.

Bob is also an Adjunct Professor at the University of Minnesota Carlson School of Management's Supply Chain and Operations Management department and at the Rutgers University School of Business Executive Education programs.

Bob earned both his MBA and bachelor's degrees from the University of St. Thomas in St. Paul, Minnesota.

Contacts And Links

Website: *www.innovativecx.com*

Podcast Series: *https://linktr.ee/AllThingsConsideredCX*

LinkedIn Profile: *www.linkedin.com/in/robertazmanmba*

Seeing Through The Smoke

David Wales CCXP MSc FRSA

The flames never used to bother me, it was the smoke, always the smoke, that made the job so much more difficult. Smoke obscures and obstructs, making it difficult to see or reach the fire, wasting valuable energy and resource along the way.

In 2009, I was enjoying a successful career in the fire and rescue service, combining my dream role as manager of the fire investigation team with attending emergencies as an officer. Both functions required extensive technical knowledge and practical competence, with potentially serious consequences for getting it wrong. It had taken over twenty years of learning, experience as well as the input of hundreds of colleagues and other experts for me to reach that point. Behind this, was the simple and well-intentioned belief, that the better I learnt my job, the better I could serve the public.

And yet, it took one person less than an hour to completely shatter this understanding and change the course of my career. How?

Because, shockingly, theirs was a voice I had not truly heard before, that of our ultimate customer, the public. They told me about how they experienced an emergency and its aftermath. Not as a series of technical procedures to extinguish a fire, but as an emotional event and one which had a very personal, and often long lasting, impact.

One which had only just begun, and far from ended, as we pulled away leaving them alone to come to terms with the consequences.

This revelation came about during what would become a pioneering national study of human behaviour in fires. I had instigated the research as we wanted to reduce the number of injuries associated with house fires. We knew that large numbers of people were not following our advice to 'get out' when encountering a fire in the home and assumed that was the problem. We believed that if we learnt enough about what they were doing, we could then change the publics' behaviours to conform to our guidance. We were, after all, the professionals, the experts.

During a six-year period, our research provided so many fascinating and diverse stories. But one lady's account struck a particular chord. Since then I have re-told it often and, more than any other, it was responsible for helping many of my colleagues understand why we needed to re-think what we did and how we did it.

So what did she tell me? Well, about eight months prior to my visit, there had been a small fire in the electrical meter cabinet located on the outside of her home, near the main door. It was caused by some work being undertaken by engineers working on the electrical supply nearby. Fortunately, the fire did not develop beyond the cabinet, but it did produce smoke, some of which found its way indoors. She explained to me:

"My eleven-year-old son was at home during the fire and is now concerned that it could happen again and that he did not respond appropriately. It would have been helpful, if you could have sent someone to have a chat to discuss this and reassure him."

When I offered to arrange this, she said it was too late now.

From our perspective, both operationally and as a data record, the fire was minor and inconsequential, easily forgotten.

And yet for the family its repercussions were ongoing. The son did not want to be left at home alone but did not always want to go out with his mum. The sight, sound or smell of any fire or smoke quickly took him back to the traumatic event. This association could haunt him for years, if not life.

And yet, it did not have to be this way. The lady knew how we could help her son but had not been offered the chance to tell us. As a result, we had missed an opportunity to turn harm to good. Had we sat down with the son, we could have explained that the fire was very unusual, unlikely to happen again and reassured him he did everything right. Had we then given him a badge or made him an honorary fire fighter, he could have gone to school and shared the fire safety message with his peers. A group that was difficult for us to reach. Who knows, he could even have gone on to become a fire safety champion or decided on a career with us.

Stories such as these (and there were many) came as a real surprise, particularly because at every stage of my career I had direct contact with customers, first as a fire fighter, and then as an officer and fire investigator. More than that, I had worked in our community safety team where we sought to know and engage with the public to help prevent fires. But it occurred to me that our relationship with, and knowledge of, the public reflected an inside-out view. We saw and recorded what we deemed to be important, and so the public were a source of one-way information. When they had knowledge we wanted, we would ask them. If not, we did not seek their views.

As a result, our worldview was formed by multiple assumptions and biases embedded randomly over time. This meant we saw and observed largely what we expected and with no moderating factor, such as a strong voice of the customer. These became self-perpetuating as we continued to put the same data through the same processes. We meant well, but it became increasingly clear that was not enough.

This made me really step back and reflect on our purpose.

If it was simply to extinguish the fire as a functional activity, then we did that. That was certainly a legitimate way to interpret our role as reflected in the relevant legislation, governance and other corporate drivers. The service was organised around these and had systems in place to ensure delivery against their various requirements. However, if we were to take a more human and customer-informed view of the experience and the harm fires did, then there would be a vastly different set of needs to deliver against.

A good example of this was quickly revealed during the first phase of our research, where we spoke to ten people using semi-structured interviews. Each of these had recently experienced a small fire in their home during which they incurred a minor injury. We asked them to tell us their story in their own words. Of the ten, eight were pet owners and seven stated that concern for their pet was the strongest driver of their behaviour during the event. This meant they had acted instinctively and, in each case, against our advice to 'get out'. Their language and tone really emphasised the powerful influence of pets. For many, a pet was their only companion and they afforded it a status no different to a person. This had significant implications in terms of their behaviour and, importantly, their satisfaction with our service based on our response to their concerns and how we treated their pet. In hindsight, pets seemed an obvious factor to consider. And yet, it took a customer to tell us.

Even at this early stage of the study, the transformative power of hearing our customers voice, direct and unconstrained, quickly became apparent. That sense of awe never changed for me, even years later, as every successive phase of research generated more insights that challenged my professional and learned assumptions.

The research was and continues to be influential on thinking and practice in the UK and internationally. It shone a light on every part of our existing organisation, leading to changes in our campaigns, call handling, operational response, and HR processes amongst others. It identified new services that were required, most notably the need for post-fire support. But it also emphasised that how the services were delivered mattered just as much, the role of empathy and emotion being critical. That was emphasised time and time again during the many workshops I ran for colleagues. These provided a powerful means for us to robustly, but sensitively, explore the issues. These triggered a lot of personal reflection with lasting mindset and behavioural change amongst attendees.

At a more fundamental level, it also raised questions about how to align, the often static and technical top-down requirements of legislative, regulatory, and other governance instruments with the more dynamic and bottom-up human level customer requirements.

Alongside the human behaviour study, we also commissioned a local university to identify how data moved through our organisation. They looked at the design, guidance, interpretation, coding, analysis, and presentation of our primary incident recording form (electronic). They identified that human factors influenced and modified these as they progressed through each stage.

In fact, beyond all the individual findings, two themes were ever present. The human experience of our customers and the highly influential but often unrecognised (or ignored) human factors that influenced our organisation in its relationship with customers and the services we provided.

I use the term human experience rather than customer or employee, because throughout our research, the wider context within which events took place were always critical to our customers experience and outcomes. They were humans first, and customers second, and I think this may be one of the most important distinctions. Why? Whilst acknowledging the role of tools such as segmenting, profiling and customer personas, these often assume a stable pattern of behaviours or traits. Real life is far messier and variable with our emotions and behaviours continually changed by external factors, such as the current state of relationships, health and finances. In our interviews, the circumstances at the time of the event were always highly relevant to the customers experience and its impact. These cannot be predicted and could only be discovered through conversation.

From my years of studying the alignment between human behaviour and organisational policies I have taken away two guiding principles.

Number one being that we are humans first, and organisations would gain much by recognising this as the true start point for designing experiences. From human, to customer, to employee, to brand. Many models currently work the other way around, and as we found, this can create a huge blind spot and seriously impair the ability to engage with, or meet your customer's real, not assumed, needs. This means embracing the ever-present variability, ambiguity and complexity of their lives, rather than constantly seeking false certainty. Understanding your customers' fears and perception of risk are essential tasks in experience design.

Secondly, there are many organisations where meeting various imposed obligations (for example, legislation, professional standards or codes of practice) can drive much of the corporate focus and activity. As these are often accompanied by various monitoring, reporting or inspection regimes, they are not ignored and can be all-consuming. The customer rarely has the same level of corporate visibility or influence. Whilst many organisations have got away with this, we now stand facing a vastly different future. One driven by changing customer expectations and technology advances.

Which brings me back to the smoke. Without the appropriate strategy and tactics, a lot of time and resources can be lost trying to locate the fire in a smoke-filled environment. You can aim water from a distance at the glow, but it is unlikely to be effective. Instead, you need to get close enough to understand the fire and apply the right medium and technique.

But smoke is also a good analogy for the organisational layers that place distance between the company and customer. It was only when I sat with customers, on their terms, and heard their story in their words, that I understood the gap between my experience as a professional and theirs as a customer. The difference between fighting a fire as a job and experiencing an unwanted fire as a member of the public. For me, this insight transformed everything, and revealed countless ways in which we could better truly help our customers, and not just do our job as we perceived it.

It is important that organisations meet their various corporate obligations and strive to improve how they perform. However, if that requires so much time and resource that customer experience is limited to being viewed through an inside-out, data led and functional lens, then you will never truly understand or engage them. Any attempt to do so will only be partially effective at best.

The world is changing rapidly and now is the time to be really close to your customers, and not just faintly perceive them through the smoke.

About David Wales CCXP MSc FRSA

David is the Founder of SharedAim, a company established to help organisations deliver excellent customer experience and enhance organisational performance. It provides a focus on human experience, human factors and being able to thrive amidst complexity and uncertainty.

Prior to this, David had a distinguished career in the Fire and Rescue Service (FRS), where he instigated and led an award-winning national study of human behaviour in fires. His insights provided an entirely new perspective, changing thinking and practice in the UK and internationally. As a result, he was appointed as the first Customer Experience Manager in the FRS, culminating in an award to acknowledge his innovation.

David continues his association with the international crisis and disaster sector, advocating the benefits of user-centred design and CX to transform services.

An award-winning presenter and researcher, he was recently recognised as one of the UK's top 50 CX influencers.

Contacts And Links

Email: *david@sharedaim.co.uk*

Website: *www.sharedaim.co.uk*

LinkedIn: *www.linkedin.com/in/davidatsharedaim*

Bring Your Customer Insights To Life With Immersion Experiences

Serena Riley

Think back to a time when you learned a valuable lesson. What do you remember about the environment? Can you recall who you were with, what you saw, or how you felt? I'm betting this lesson wasn't learned through a set of spoken or written words, but through a memorable experience you've internalized. As a mom of three kids, I have expended plenty of energy suggesting actions my kids should take to avoid painful situations, which often go unheard. It's not until a toy that was left out gets broken or pizza spontaneously combusts because the microwave timer was set to three minutes instead of 30 seconds, that the feedback is fully absorbed and the lesson locked into memory - until then, it was just mom spewing nonsense.

"Learning is an experience. Everything else is just information"
– Albert Einstein

We know that understanding our customers is foundational to our CX strategy. Most CX professionals begin their path to understanding by constructing a Customer Journey Map (CJM), but what do we do with it once it is complete? How do we create greater organizational understanding, customer empathy, and a business case for change? Stick with me through this chapter as I share how I designed immersive experiences born from CJM insights to generate positive change by exposing our employees to the same emotional triggers our customers experienced.

While it's typically easy to *see* where improvement opportunities exist when examining our CJMs, it's not always easy to gain agreement and/or alignment from the rest of the organization as to the importance, prioritization, and potential resource spend of said improvements. One method I found extremely helpful to combat these challenges was to produce employee-attended immersion experience sessions. These low-cost learning experiences have the potential to reap priceless benefits.

When crafting an immersion experience, you should focus on highlighting the current state of one of your CJM's micro-journeys requiring improvement. You want this to be an as-close-to-reality simulation as possible, allowing the employees to develop the same thoughts and feelings your customers do when traveling this micro-journey. Once you have determined which micro-journey to simulate, use the following six considerations to design your session:

1. Experience Requirements. The same intentional design methodologies used for crafting our customer experiences need to be employed when designing immersion experiences. To create the most successful results, these experiences should be:

- **Interactive** to engage your employees and keep their attention.
- **Informative** to give your employees new and actionable data points.
- **Immersive** to provide your employees a safe and authentic space to truly feel your customers' experiences.

2. Experience Objectives. What are the emotions or sentiments your customers have expressed? What qualitative and quantitative data do you have that supports these sentiments? You want your employees to think, feel, see, and do the same things as your customers would throughout the session.

3. Experience Hosts. Who are the appropriate parties that should lead this session? Who will bring the needed energy and influence to making this an impactful event? Do not underestimate the host's role - you want someone(s) who can bring the experience to life, share their passion for the customer, and inspire the attendees to act on the outcomes. This is an opportune time to include employees who support the backend processes (IT, Customer Support, Call Center, etc.) - allow them to participate and simulate the aspect of the experience they support so employees get an even more comprehensive understanding of the full experience.

4. Experience Structure. Who is your target audience of attendees? Who would gain the most from attending this session and stepping into the customer's shoes? What is the appropriate session length to keep the audience engaged while still providing the greatest impact?

5. Experience Materials. What access, documentation, websites, software, hardware, etc. do your customers need to complete this micro-journey? Are there any prerequisites the audience must complete before attending? How will you deliver this session - will it be in-person, remote, or a hybrid? You will want to assure any materials needed to execute the micro-journey are prepared and available for use during - and before, if necessary - the session.

6. Experience Marketing. What internal channels of communication can you tap into to promote this session? Who are your allies and champions within your audience that can help share the value of attending this session? Since you are commandeering a portion of your audience's calendar, you need to ensure the marketing of this event sparks enthusiasm and sets expectations as to the value to be gained from attending.

While it may seem like a lot to contemplate, the more deliberate your strategy and planning of this session, the more value you will deliver. The more value you deliver, the more excitement will build around these, and future, sessions. And the more excitement you build around these sessions, the more customer obsession will flourish.

So, how do you pull all these thoughts together into a cohesive agenda? Below is a simple six-point template I developed and use for the events I produce. I typically try to keep the session length to 60-minutes, but you may need to adjust depending on the complexity of the micro-journey.

1. **Introduction.** Get the party started! Set the energy and expectations. This is a good time to remind the audience what CX is and the value it brings to each employee's job function and to the overall organization. Then give a brief overview (save the details for the immersion) of the micro-journey you'll be exploring.
2. **Pre-Immersion Live Polling.** Engage the audience and gauge their expectations. Use a live polling tool to measure, in real-time, what the audience expects this micro-journey experience to be (e.g., "Enter one word/phrase that describes what your expectations are of the <enter micro-journey name here>.").
Capture a screenshot of the results for use in Step 5.
3. **Micro-Journey Immersion.** Provide the technology, tools, and materials to simulate the micro-journey, as if they were the

customer. Depending on the complexity of this micro-journey, you may need to shorten the immersion to fit into the time allotted - just be sure not to leave out any salient parts of the experience.

- **Tip #1:** Here's where you will find tremendous benefit having your internal support employees present (e.g., IT, Customer Support, Call Center, etc.) to help attendees as they potentially struggle through the immersion. It will give attendees first-hand visibility to what those teams go through to support customers, validating the importance of good customer service.

- **Tip #2:** Remember to have fun with it to make it more memorable. In one immersion, we gave attendees buzzers to hit when they encountered a problem. Not only did it create a sensory cue to emphasize the frustration of having a problem, but they also had to wait for a member of the customer support team to help them, just like our customers do.

4. **Post-Immersion Live Polling.** Re-engage and regauge the audience's reality. Use a live polling tool to measure, in real-time, the audience's reality of this micro-journey experience (e.g., "Enter one word / phrase that describes what you thought/ felt during the immersion."). Capture a screenshot of the results for use in Step 5.

5. **Guided CJM Tour.** Share the digital copy of your Customer Journey Map, zooming in on the area that represents the micro-journey explored in this session. Show what your customers' expectations are and compare to those your audience shared in Step 2 - they should be similar, if not the same. Guide them through the journey, which should mirror the immersion the audience just completed. Finally, review the customer emotions and sentiments and compare them to those your audience shared in Step 4 - again, they should be similar, if not the same.

6. **Closing.** This is a great time to ask the audience to brainstorm suggestions for ways to improve the micro-journey. It is also a convenient moment to review any projects or initiatives that are in progress to address the pain points and communicate how the audience can support them.

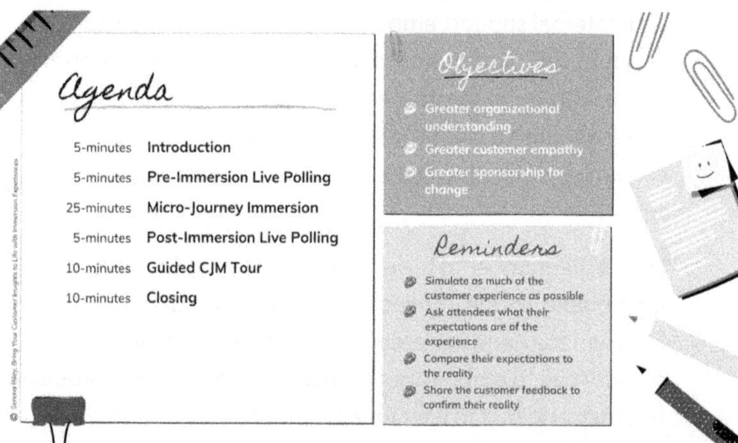

At the conclusion of this session, your employees should have a deeper understanding of your customers' experience within the chosen micro-journey as well as a realization or reminder of how their roles impact the journey.

How could such a seemingly simple and inexpensive immersive experience provide such benefits? If it is not clear already, here are some of the positive outcomes I have observed from leading these events:

- **Awareness** of CX principles, the value they provide, and how these experiences relate to employees and their roles. Business unit leaders saw the value and invited us into more conversations to provide additional visibility to CX insights.
- **Appreciation** for the customer experiences AND the employees who serve and support customers. More of the customer insights were retained, employees recognized more of the work done by internal teams to support customers, and word-of-mouth recommendations for these sessions brought new interest to the field of CX.

- **Advocacy** for delivering better experiences based on insights gleaned from customers, and new CX relationships from individual allies / champions and business unit partnerships. The empathy and engagement from the immersion experiences established buy-in for prioritization and resource spend on projects or initiatives designed to address customer pain points.
- **Assessment** for gathering additional experience feedback and taking a real-time look at the effects of the spotlighted customer experience. Employees' feedback about their experience helped identify potential improvements, emboldening them to be a part of the solution.

As CX professionals, we know how critical, yet difficult, it can be to evangelize change. The more we empower employees to be the change we want to see, the greater the impact we will be able to make. Creating interactive and engaging immersion experiences benefits everyone in the room, and more importantly, those not in the room - customers.

So, if you find yourself struggling to get your organization to take action on customer insights, bring the information to life. Use your Customer Journey Map as a catalyst for spreading customer-centricity throughout your organization by bringing your employees closer to your customers, enabling positive change for all.

About Serena Riley, CCXP

Serena Riley is a Certified Customer Experience Professional (CCXP) who has been igniting transformation in individuals, teams, and organizations for over 15-years. She is a customer experience expert who specializes in cultivating customer-centricity and employee-elevation. Her passionate positivity and creative flair have enabled organizations to drive solution and experience improvements, increasing engagement and delivering happiness to customers and employees.

Serena is an active member in the Customer Experience Professionals Association (CXPA) and Michigan's Association of Customer Experience Professionals (CXofM). In 2020, she earned CXofM's Individual Award for the Advancement of CX and CXPA's CX Impact Award. These awards recognize her leadership of organizational CX efforts and inspiring excellence in all aspects of the CX discipline.

Contacts And Links

Website: *https://www.msserenariley.com*

LinkedIn: *https://www.linkedin.com/in/serenariley*

Facebook: *https://www.facebook.com/joy.and.moxie*

Instagram: *https://www.instagram.com/joy.and.moxie*

Who Do You Think You're Talking To?

Anita Ellis

What if marketing was motivated by a desire to serve, not sell?

To assist, not advertise? To help, not hype?

How would a shift in the fundamental purpose behind marketing communications, affect a customer's overall perception of your brand?

Customer Experience (CX) is so often the focus for interactions during the purchase and usage phases of the customer life cycle. But, if perception is synonymous with experience, you can impact CX long before a customer becomes a customer. And, if emotions are at the heart of how we perceive brands, putting customers first at the stage of need can enhance this connection and their experience.

You could assume, I suppose, that if marketing is successful in generating a lead or converting a customer, the experience must have been good. But, does a lead or conversion from a piece of marketing indicate a customer centric approach, or did the customer simply choose the least worst available option? Most importantly, does it matter?

If your cost of acquisition is high, then yes. If your retention rates are low, then yes.

Meaningful marketing that shows you care or helps the

customer in some way, can emotionally connect a customer to your brand and service because it shows (rather than tells) the customer you value them.

We saw a surge in these kind of communications in 2020. United by the pandemic, banks emailed customers to say; "Don't worry about your overdraft this month". Retailers marketed discounts for keyworkers without deadlines or conditions attached. Social campaigns were full of genuine help, advice and free activities for the kids. These communications struck a chord because the emotion was real. The motivation behind the marketing had the customer at its core. With a genuine desire to help.

Putting The Customer At The Heart Of Your Marketing And Communications

How then, can you ensure your marketing is motivated by a desire to help and put the customer first?

In my experience, customers want three things:

- A clear understanding of what's in it for them (it's not about you)
- Transparency; tell it like it is and don't hide anything (customers will see through it)
- To be inspired and delighted (everyone loves a happy ending)

Marketing communications, whether at the awareness, acquisition, conversion or retention stage, have the power to do all three.

1. It's Not About You

It has always fascinated me how some companies have a natural tendency to craft communications that talk more about themselves than to their customers. More 'we' than 'you'.

More 'our' than 'your'. More 'here you go' than 'here to help'. In an attempt to explain a service, we can overlook how the customer might experience the information we are trying to impart.

Websites can be notoriously 'company-first' in their communication style. Because content is often written in-house. And employees, no matter how knowledgeable, are focused on the 'we'. It's not just small companies. Over the years, I've been surprised at how many large, multi-national companies don't talk *to* their customers on their biggest piece of real estate.

In order for a customer to feel understood and, at the same time, understand what's in it for them, a communication has to resonate deeply. It needs to answer the problem you can help them to solve. Their pain point. Their sleep-preventing predicament. It sounds so obvious. And it's the basis of marketing best-practice the world over, but still, so much marketing falls short of accurately articulating the customer's problem.

I recently worked with a telecommunications company desperate to save their customers money and simultaneously make their lives easier. They were genuinely trying to help their customers, but attempts to communicate this and incite change had fallen flat. Why? Because their communications were (unintentionally) all about them and their solution. They hadn't emotionally connected with the customer and the customer's problem. So, customers weren't emotionally motivated.

The answer? Pop on the customers' boots. Mud and all. I interviewed their customers to identify key and pressing issues. Then we created a set of communications almost exclusively about the customer, demonstrating a deep understanding of the problem, a genuine desire to help and a story of an organisation in the same boat (more on the impact of case studies later!).

2. Seeing Through A Lack Of Transparency

I'm a big believer in being upfront in communications. There's nothing more customer-centric than telling it like it is (even if it's a perceived negative). I also think honesty is under-rated and everything can be improved with a little transparency. If your service or industry is known as being quite dull, acknowledge it. And use the unexpected reaction as a springboard for an open and honest conversation about why. If a document is full of legal but necessary details, embrace it. And use it as a point of difference to enhance the customer's experience. If you drive your customers to distraction with all the questions you need to ask, admit it. And make it a positive and valuable experience.

Customers will see through a lack of transparency. Holding back information or miscommunication is the cause of a lot of customer dissatisfaction. Consider these all too common examples of companies attempting to conceal: the 'contains important documents' direct mail tactic, the 'contact us' circus trying everything to avoid contact of any kind, the web chat pretending to answer your question but not actually imparting any information, the website filled with acronyms and corporate nonsense that no-one understands (not even the people who wrote it), and the unsubscribe link hidden for fear of being found (and used).

These are all examples of marketing that is hiding something, in case it puts off a customer. Which is does anyway because the concealment is so obvious. So obvious in fact that putting 'Please don't read' on that direct mail envelope might get a better reaction.

A couple of months ago, something unexpected happened. I'd started working with Hartsfield, a UK-based financial services company. We'd been working on a series of advertorials, and I'd been interviewing employees and directors to find out more about financial wellbeing. Since I'm usually the one asking; 'what's in it for the customer?' or encouraging the client to make their communications all about the customer, I was pleasantly surprised when the directors told me they wanted to transform their client compliance agreement and make it more customer friendly. This was music to my CX ears. Not only did they aim to make every part of the document clear and easy to understand (no jargon, no complex terminology, no acronyms); they wanted the document to feel like a conversation and to be as enjoyable as possible to read.

This level of transparency and focus on the customer experience is motivated by a desire to help and to make things easy for customers. Which is part of their ethos. But it's not just empty rhetoric; they reinforce their customer-centric culture by making that the foundation of their communications.

3. A Happy Ending

Every piece of marketing communication has the power to emotionally connect with the customer and therefore to delight. Even the most mundane. Like creative cookie statements that lessen the pain of those annoying pop-ups. Client agreements or policy documents that acknowledge their yawn-inducing properties with a touch of self-deprecation. Technical products or services refreshingly free from jargon. A carefully crafted email that draws a smile. Each communication contributes to the intangible perception and experience of your company.

Customers want to feel excited at the prospect of working with you. Or at least relieved you're solving their problem. From the initial marketing emails they receive, to the follow-up after a sales call, or the celebratory email following implementation, all these pieces of communication can affect how the customer feels.

In order to have truly customer-centric communications, you need to be crystal clear on who you are talking to. To emotionally connect, you need to take your audience on a journey. This is where the power of storytelling can put the customer at the heart of your marketing.

I hate the term case study. It sounds so clinical and uninspiring. But a story? Now you've got me. Stories make things memorable. They can create an emotional connection with your customer and therefore affect their experience.

Case studies or customer stories, when written in the right way, are relevant, meaningful, and aspirational all at the same time.

I don't mean perfunctory descriptions of solutions you delivered for a similar customer. Or a list of services you implemented. I mean a story-style approach that connects with a customer because they immediately identify with the problem, understand what's in it for them, and are inspired to make a change.

When a case study represents your target audience, it's highly relevant. If it accurately describes a real pain point, it will resonate. When you have achieved real results for your customer, the reader will aspire to achieve the same. A piece of communication that is relevant, meaningful, and aspirational can dramatically impact a customer's perception and therefore their experience.

The better the experience, the easier it is to get testimonials and case studies and so it becomes cyclical. Your customer-focused approach creates loyal customers who are advocates and happy to be used as cases studies; case studies that are the true voice of the customer and highlight a positive experience; an experience which others aspire to, which in turn creates more customers.

Ultimately, showing you care with customer-centric, boldly transparent and delight-inducing communications goes a long way to enhancing a customer's perception and experience, creating brand advocates that contribute to positive business performance.

About Anita Ellis

Anita Ellis is a passionate storyteller, marketing consultant and copywriter. She is a certified marketer and founder and director of copywriting agency Lexicomm where she helps innovative brands stand-out with creative, customer-focused communications.

When she's not immersed in case studies, Anita can be found getting creative in the kitchen or devouring the dictionary to win at Scrabble.

Contacts And Links

Email: *anita@lexicomm.co.uk*

Web: *www.lexicomm.co.uk*

Facebook: *https://www.facebook.com/Lexicomm*

Linked In: *https://www.linkedin.com/in/anitaellis*

The Eclectic Customer – Humanized Customer Experience

Miles Courtney-Thomas

Imagine just for a moment that companies could view customers from a higher level of consciousness, to perceive, understand and contextualise them within their own realities. In this chapter I will discuss a missing piece of the puzzle in terms of how companies both build understanding of customers and build awareness of the importance of customer success in a more eclectic and holistic way.

Now, please bear with me as I delve into this topic as I may stray into psychological, philosophical and slightly esoteric ramblings but I promise, you won't be disappointed.

As humans, we experience the world through our senses such as taste, smell, sight, hearing and touch. These sensory inputs allow us to interpret the world around us and it is this data which allows us to form thoughts, feelings and opinions. The output here manifests into observable behaviours and actions.

Yes, humans (we) are amazing, we are complicated and not always rational in our thinking, but our lives are rich and full of experiences both good and bad. We are certainly much more than simply the interactions we have with companies. We are all on our own journeys looking for success and happiness. If companies were able to achieve a more holistic understanding of customers in this broader context there could be significant opportunities for innovation and disruption while building higher levels of advocacy.

The world changed for us all due to the devastation caused by the pandemic but what has also changed is our expectations of companies, namely we have a greater need for them to understand us and we want them to play a more active role in making the world a better place.

The big question is; Are companies aware of this change in the collective mindset? Do they understand the opportunities that greater understanding of customers in a human concept can bring?

Today, companies view customers through a siloed lens, one that is driven by product and services rather than real-life. In other words, companies build understanding of customers from an 'inner track' perspective rather than the Gestaltian 'outer track' for which the whole is greater than the sum of its parts. Companies are mostly only involved in one step of an end-to-end experience.

I posit here that the companies that are able to elucidate understanding of broader and more holistic views of the customer (societal impact and responsibility) will be the leaders of the future. I will be providing some real-life examples of where I have (rarely) seen this happen and share some insights and inspiration based on my thinking about how we can make a better world through improving customer experiences.

There are two distinct but related disciplines within customer experience that, when evolved, could produce a significant step change in the way companies operate.

1. Voice of the customer (VOC): this is used by companies to help build an understanding of customers and their needs and drivers by listening in multiple ways.

2. Customer Success: this is designed to help anticipate needs and support the customer in gaining the maximum value from their investment in the technology, this is most often used by Software as a Service (SaaS) companies.

Voice Of The Customer

The focus of most VOC programmes is limited to understanding the experience based on the current journeys and services that have been designed for them, this is what I term the 'inner track' or blinkered knowledge. While this may help make tweaks or improvements in products or services, it is unlikely to help in the creation of either disruptive innovation or meet the needs of customers within this context.

Customer Success

Similarly, customer success programmes are focused on allowing the customer to gain the greatest value or success when using the tool without an appreciation of the wider real-life journeys which may provide significant insight and opportunity.

These current approaches are valuable as they are, but I believe that we should seek to evolve these approaches to take a more holistic human view.

Both Customer Success and Voice of the Customer typically focus on the 'inside track', this means that the core focus is on building understanding of the customer and planning for their success within the narrow context of the companies' services or products and/or ensuring the customer achieves their goals when using their technology.

The Problem

The problem is that they have only a limited, a partial perception. To illustrate this risk, I'll now to jump into the philosophical and a somewhat esoteric analysis as promised.

Hopefully, there are some Plato fans here as I will attempt to briefly draw an analogy using Plato's Allegory of the Cave. In this allegory, he ruminates about the perception of reality.

Plato describes a person who is chained facing a wall in a cave. Behind this person, there is a fire and between the fire and the person there are people walking which creates shadows on the wall. The shadows the person sees on the wall are perceived as real people based on a partial perception of reality. As I mentioned earlier, our senses form our thoughts and opinions, a partial view of reality restricts our capability to evolve, innovate and reason. This will also direct our behaviours based on a flawed understanding of the environment.

One day, this person escapes the chains and turns around to see the fire and the people in their true form. At this point, one's understanding of reality is irreversibly altered and a higher-level understanding is achieved and as a consequence/result, new opportunities immediately present themselves. Just wait until this person walks out of the cave and sees the sun for the first time!

Companies are currently chained to an approach which sees them focus on a small facet of the whole (myopic), which is hampering their ability to understand customers (or broader societal issues) in a more eclectic or holistic manner. As Gestalt would say, 'the whole is greater than the sum of its parts'.

This, for me, is an important missing piece. The customer is more than just someone that interacts with your products or services. As a human, they have their own values and their own past, which they use to build expectations for future experiences, they are also impacted by situations at a global and societal level which can influence their use of your services; this is the 'outside track'. You need to care about these pressures, be seen to understand they exist and be supportive and helpful in a broader context.

A Real-Life Example

Let me jump in with a real-life example. I was recently acting as a judge for the customer experience awards and one of the entries was from a vehicle renting firm.

Once lockdown took hold, they were understandably concerned about the survival of the company, as many customers may choose not to move ahead with rentals. The company understood the broader concern of the customer in relation to the societal impact. Specifically, many customers did not know if they would be furloughed or even lose their jobs.

Their need for a vehicle remained, but they were concerned that if they lost their income, they would then be unable to pay. By understanding the context and concern of customers beyond the 'inner track', they were able to innovate for this specific concern by including income protection insurance with every rental contract. As a result, sales were not only maintained but instead exceeded projections which were made before the impact of COVID-19 was known. Even better, they enabled customer success in achieving goals despite the global situation. This is where real innovation and customer advocacy happens.

Now, this change did not necessarily come about from a conscious awareness of the need to understand the context of the customer more broadly. It was likely as a result of trying to react to an issue but you can see here how building a more holistic understanding can lead to innovation and advocacy. The best and most courageous ideas often come from the need to make a decision in difficult circumstances

I've also seen many companies providing updates on the pandemic situation to their customers as they understand it is having an impact and causes concern. This is good of course but doesn't go far enough within the framework of this topic. There are some organisations today who do this, but they tend to be charities, not-for-profit, patient-led companies or housing associations. They are led by a mission statement which often is very human in nature and which has a real focus on well-being.

Let's take the example of housing associations. Their key focus is providing affordable housing, but we do see they go much further than this by providing access to debt charities and advice, producing videos or guides on how to run a budget, how to request housing benefit and what to do if you have anti-social problems in the neighbourhood. These are what I would call value-added ancillary services within the ecosystem that help in support of the broader mission, which is usually around the right to have a happy home.

We need to understand where customers have been, where they are and where they want to go.

Three Types

There are three main types of companies within this construct:

1. **Inner track (traditional) companies.** They look purely at directly correlating interactions with their company and its services.
2. **Mid track (Advancing) companies.** They look for opportunities with ancillary services, where they can bring added value through a greater appreciation of the customer in a broader yet related sense.
3. **Outer track (Innovating) companies.** They have developed initiatives to understand the eclectic customer in ways that are not necessarily ancillary nor connected to current products and services but rather though seeking to understand them at a human and societal level and their values.

Outer track companies hold a significant advantage and, aside from the above, tend to have a social conscience; they lead by example, are not afraid to hold a position on issues facing the wider world and society and build advocacy through being seen to want to make the world a better place. It is also their understanding of a customer on a real-life journey that can allow them to make disruptive and innovative change happen.

And Finally

Simply put, customers are appreciative of a wider understanding of their concerns and values. Those companies that seek to enable customer success in the broader meaning and those that are seen to 'do good' for the benefit of society are the ones who will ultimately triumph. Not only through building genuine advocacy and respect but also by innovating and acting as a differentiator.

It's time for companies to step up and to help us in creating a better world

I'll leave you with a quote.

"Intelligence without empathy is an empty path."
Miles C. Thomas

About Miles Courtney-Thomas

Miles is a seasoned customer service and experience expert having worked in the field for many years. Miles is also a certified CX professional who believes in the importance of taking a human approach to the delivery of great service and experiences.

He is a customer experience judge and chair of judges in industry awards and has also been named as a global leader and influencer in the CX sphere by Customer Experience Magazine and My Customer Magazine among others. Miles is the founder of Humanized CX and CX Wales.

His experience in technology, service and experience combined with a degree in Psychology has provided a unique lens in humanizing the customer experience.

Views expressed in this chapter are his own

Contacts And Links

www.humanizedcx.com

www.cxwales.com

https://www.linkedin.com/in/milesct/

https://twitter.com/milescthomas

4.CX Design And Improvement

Creating experiences that engage customers and employees alike

The Journey Makes The Experience

James Brooks

Why The Journey Is As Important As The Outcome

Great customer service must be focussed on consistently delivering the right outcome for the customer. Delivered through an experience which is truly engaging, pro-actively manages expectations, and positively differentiates the organisation from it's competitors.

Simply enabling a host of functions to be accessed online won't translate to high-levels of customer engagement, self service or customer satisfaction. The route the customer takes to reach the destination is as important as the final outcome.

In some cases, the journey itself is the reason for wanting to get to the destination. Think London to New York flying on Concorde. The exclusivity and luxury combined with the supersonic speed of travel was often the reason for making the trip in the first place.

This isn't suggesting every customer journey needs to be as lavish as a transatlantic jaunt aboard Concorde but, perhaps they should be as innovative. I think most people would be satisfied with a budget airline cabin if London to New York took just three hours instead of seven.

Removing The Barrier To Entry

Has society become lazy or have expectations increased? I think the answer is expectations are higher, so people can choose leisure over labour.

One of the most overlooked aspects of every customer journey is how customers access the journey. Signposting people to your website is not enough.

If the customer must move their body beyond raising their phone to their line of sight, you've lost them. They are not getting up to grab their laptop just to interact with you. They're not even going to raise their hand to their ear to call you unless it's a transaction that they absolutely must complete.

We're living in an era of immediacy. Convenience. Most people value time above all else. We'll pay more for a better experience, or to endure a less hellish one. Or we just won't do business at all if the journey becomes remotely difficult.

Customers may be willing to invest more effort when the outcome promotes an emotive response, like making a significant purchase. However, with ever increasing market saturation, it's the experience leading up to the purchase which will differentiate you from your competitors.

You should be designing customer journeys that fit in and around people's lifestyles. Seamless customer experiences that don't require people to leave their leisure bubble.

Right now mobile is king. It's more than just accessing your website from a mobile device, the transaction must be 'tap, tap, swipe' optimised. Additionally, mobile messaging apps are some of the most highly consumed mobile applications in use. You should be considering how you can deliver customer journeys conversationally through a mixture of automation, live advisor, and the asynchronous messaging habits of consumers today.

Voice is also gathering pace rapidly. Being able to talk to your devices and appliances. Not just talking to your phone, or even your smart speakers, but talking to your TV, fridge-freezer, and your car. This is truly the definition of inserting customer experiences into a person's lifestyle. If you're in the kitchen waiting for the coffee to brew, why shouldn't you be able to ask the fridge "when is my grocery delivery due?" It's about giving the customer the option to act on their own terms, at their convenience.

A Practical Example: Water Company – Change Of Address

Updating a customer address is one of the highest reasons for contact for numerous organisations, in particular utilities and service providers.

A typical mistake is to identify the key components of the journey based solely on what you as the organisation need to capture from the customer, instead of considering what the customer needs from you in order to complete the journey successfully.

Let's step through the end to end process from the customer's perspective and at each stage identify opportunities to make the experience easier, more intuitive and informative.

Step 1: Starting The Journey

Customer searches for your website online.

- **Opportunity #1:** Does your Search Engine Optimisation (SEO) create search results with page links for your highest volume reasons for contact? e.g. I'm moving house.
- **Opportunity #2:** For customers that go directly to your homepage, are there clear unmissable links or buttons for customers to quickly access the highest reasons for contact?
- **Opportunity #3:** Is your website optimised for different mobile devices, screen sizes and browsers? Customers should be able to

engage with you online using whatever device they've invested in and their preferred browser.

This journey is happening through necessity. It's completely transactional and in most cases the customer just wants to get in and get out. Make it easy for them to do that without an unnecessary tour of the website.

Step 2: Setting Expectations

From the organisation side, you already know what information you need from the customer. You know how long it will take to complete the process and even if the process can be completed in one go via the chosen channel, in this example the website. The customer doesn't know anything at this point - so tell them!

In our example customer journey, one of the key factors required to complete the process is the final meter reading. However, there is a time dependency. If the customer is moving house in six weeks' time, you're probably not going to want the meter reading today.

- **Opportunity #1:** Qualify that the transaction can be completed now by asking for customer information in the right order. In this case, before you go any further, ask the customer when their expected move date is. If the date is outside of the threshold, advise the customer when the earliest time is that they can come back and submit their change of address. That way the customer isn't going to be left frustrated by wasting their time progressing halfway through a process only to be told it cannot be completed at this time.

- **Opportunity #2:** If it's too early for the customer to update their address, why not offer to remind them when it is time to update their address? A simple SMS or email with a URL that brings them directly into the process. One less thing for the customer to remember.

- **Opportunity #3:** Once you've confirmed the move date is inside the threshold, tell the customer up front what information they're going to need to successfully complete the process, and how long it's expected to take. Now the customer feels informed and can decide whether to proceed now or later.

Step 3: Use The Information You Already Know About The Customer

In order for the organisation to complete the change of address, it's likely you'll need to know who the customer is, an account number, current address and to confirm that the person completing this transaction is the customer themselves. All of this can be covered by simply asking the customer to log into their online account.

- **Opportunity #1:** Once the customer has authenticated by successfully accessing their online account, use the information that you already know about the customer, don't ask the customer to provide it.
- **Opportunity #2:** If you need to ask the customer for a piece of information that is going to be used multiple times throughout the process, ensure that information is retained through the process. Don't ask the customer to re-enter it multiple times. Nobody likes repeating themselves!

Step 4: Keep It Clean, Keep It Clear, Keep It Smart

Once the customer begins the transactional elements of the journey, you don't want to overwhelm them by having everything on a single page. Break down each data entry task to a single page and that way the customer won't get distracted from the task at hand.

- **Opportunity #1:** Water meters are largely standardised but there are a few different versions installed in people's homes and making sure the reading is accurate is critical.

Presenting graphics or images of different meters and explicitly highlighting which numbers make up the reading is a really easy way to remove any 'guess work' from the process.

- **Opportunity #2:** Use the native features of the customer's prized smart phone to make the whole process even easier. Give the customer the option to take a picture of their meter to capture the reading. A little Optical Character Recognition (OCR) on your part and you come out looking 'challenger bank slick!'
- **Opportunity #3:** Let the customer know how far through the process they are by displaying a progress tracker. Keep the customer motivated to get to the end.

Step 5: What Now?

So many transactional journeys leave the customer in doubt as to the success of the transaction and what happens next.

If the outcome can be verified as complete there and then, make it clear to the customer on screen – Large font and a big green tick is pretty final!

- **Opportunity #1:** With more formal transactions you might consider sending a confirmation email in addition. The customer can be doubly confident that everything was updated successfully.
- **Opportunity #2:** If for some reason the outcome cannot be verified as complete immediately or requires additional steps to be taken by the customer, present this information on screen. Be clear as to why the outcome has not been verified, how long the customer should wait before contacting the organisation to check on progress or better yet, confirm that the organisation will contact the customer directly once the outcome is complete.

Summary: Challenge Your Thinking

There will be several determining factors for the level of experience you want to be providing your customers such as service or sales, luxury or budget, emotive or not.

Before you do anything know who you are, what you're offering and understand what your customers expect. For example, customers that have signed up to your loyalty scheme have higher expectations than the one-time customer. You might consider tailoring different journeys accordingly.

There is always the temptation to construct a customer journey by dovetailing existing technical processes. In my experience every journey should be discreet to preserve the integrity of the overall experience.

No customer is going to appreciate the technical complexities happening in the background. They're solely focussed on what's in front of them. What they can see, hear and touch. The style needs to match the substance to maximise engagement.

Finally, channel selection. Whether it's mobile, desktop or voice, ensure that it's easy for you customers to get started. Be accessible through technology that your customers are comfortable with and already use frequently.

At the end of the day, the easier you are to do business with, the more business you'll do.

About James Brooks

James is a customer experience professional and leader in applied innovation.

He has over 18 years of customer engagement experience, serving in numerous operational, analytical and technology-based roles, across multiple industries and sectors.

James' current areas of focus lie in emerging and disruptive technology, human centred design, and the application of artificial intelligence to create and deliver better outcomes for customers.

Contact And Links

Email: *jamesbrooksinnovation@gmail.com*

Apple Podcasts: *https://podcasts.apple.com/gb/podcast/the-sploogle-function*

LinkedIn: *www.linkedin.com/in/james-brooks-innovation*

Spotify Podcasts: *https://open.spotify.com/show/11G7edmQ3GW4HCTdwTzBLS*

The Art And Science Of CX Process Design Powered By Interaction Intelligence Data

Daniel Dougherty

Using operational data to construct Interactional Intelligence boosts program design and shortens time to value for automation initiatives, VOC programs, and Human-Human interactions.

It's evident! Design and Data are cornerstones in one's ability to consistently accomplish desired experience outcomes.

As someone reading a book regarding the practice and application of Customer Experience (CX), you're likely familiar with the countless case studies focused on brands that invest in design-focused CX. You are probably already thinking about the ones I'm talking about, the likes of Apple, Southwest Airlines, Disney, Amazon, and Ritz Carlton.

You are aware of the meticulously designed and routinely executed CX-centered business models that place them in a class above the simply great companies. In fact, you probably have no doubt the importance of the tried-and-true CX toolkits and the part they play in the creation of these world-class cultures and Brands.

If you're not familiar, it's worth searching out. I routinely review these types of reports and have taken recent notice of two prominent themes from these differentiated experiences: 1) detail data being functional, and 2) Process design ahead of process improvement.

These themes resonate with me as I was Six Sigma, and ISO indoctrinated early in my career and formed a special bond with the discipline of measuring processes and the supporting data and calculations. This passion for process design, teamed with (a sometimes fanatical) measurement alignment, caused one of my mentors to often, and I hope at least half-jokingly, attribute many of my professional opportunities to me merely being someone with the "heart of an artist and the mind of an engineer."

Eventually, I attempted to turn this bug into a feature, knowing that CX management balances art and science. I established a few guiding principles for undertaking CX or Employee Experience (EX) initiatives. This included a principle being solely focused on leveraging the data generated by the processes themselves, something to the effect of, ***if leveraged for continuous improvement, the company's most valuable asset is the data generated during its operations.***

This "generated data" principle was a meta-approach that focused on an organization's ability to use aggregate data to detect and reduce defects impacting actual assets such as employees, customers, inventories, supply chains, properties, etc.

Yet, in the last five years, our collective ability to utilize contextual data has come online in a big way and is ushering in a new era of interaction possibilities. An era where we can apply this principle in the moment—eventually tapping the data generated by a process, during its process - right there as the interaction is happening and tuned for an audience of one.

Evolving the "generated data" principle into this new era, let's define *Interaction Intelligence as a designed usage of data categorized by:*

- The ability to extract information from an interaction to inform overall business decisions, policies, and processes.

Or

- The ability to supply context to parties (Human or Machine) during an interaction that enhances our ability to modify behaviors during that interaction.

Move Your Improvement Goals From 5% To 5X, Amplifying Design With Interactional Data

Today's macro trends have set in motion a move from digital transformation in the information age to an experience age where customers and employees will have increasingly multi-dimensional digital profiles.

Trends such as mobility, cloud, IoT, low code APIs, decreasing compute costs, and algorithm efficiency were already present, yet heavily boosted during 2020's global pandemic. Our response to the pandemic significantly accelerated both business and consumer adoption of digital transformation and pushed all generations and most market segments to become more accepting of interactions blending technology and humans.

Given the increasing number of devices and digital channels coupled with accelerated digital adoption and improvements in our ability to capture data, it becomes apparent that the amount of Interactional-level data is growing exponentially and will continue to each minute after the next.

It is intuitive that with this big interactional data comes big opportunities. Our ability to sample and model has indeed improved and our ability to root cause, but in this big data is also big noise, big bias, and big expectations.

As I see it, the opportunity lies in our ability to add valuable context, turning that data into information and, ultimately, intelligence.

Our ability to do that at scale is still in its infancy. To achieve this, we will need to rely not on data engineering and development but on people and practices from domains with deep business acumen. People with the ability to construct meaningful questions and map a path from the data needed to generate answers, along with the expertise of how to use vast touchpoints to influence human behavior and achieve the experience that meets our desired outcomes.

It's in this balance of art and science. Between intuition and algorithms, and much like navigators before us, we are beginning to advance our collective toolkits from a compass rose into a GPS-like world of precision. For now, our firm is using more of a sextant; we call data signals.

These Data Signals are aggregations of interaction elements tuned against business outcomes. They are just algorithms constructed much like classical KPIs and their measures, but the trends above allow us to create much higher fidelity and accuracy.

Ultimately, this method allows us to find patterns in very large data sets that are meaningful to small audiences. We marry those trends with operational playbooks, which produce additional data points we use to monitor anomalies and tune the processes. And that is where the art of experience design becomes enormously important.

Process Design Ahead Of Process Improvement

"It is time to stop paving the cow paths. Instead of embedding outdated processes in silicon and software, we should obliterate them and start over. We should "reengineer" our businesses: use the power of modern information technology to radically redesign our business processes in order to achieve dramatic improvements in their performance."

Hammer, M. (1990) Reengineering Work: Don't Automate, Obliterate. Harvard Business Review

This quote is from a prophetic 1990's HBR article that happens to be even more pertinent thirty years later. The article discusses how the usual methods of obtaining business outcomes have not yielded expected ROIs. I am confident if Michael Hammer were still with us, he would be equally justified and horrified at how present this is with most of today's automation and AI marketplace.

If our goal is dramatically improving experience outcomes, it is very often best to blow up what we (or our industry) may have. Starting over, developing holistically, and in the aggregate with the end in mind.

Even if we do not demolish the existing processes, we should abstract ourselves from the current, working from a clean slate on how the Brand, Customer, and Employees best fit together.

In parallel, we should consider the maturity of the processes that support our experiences and apply design thinking to them. Below is a four-level framework outlining the spectrum of that maturity.

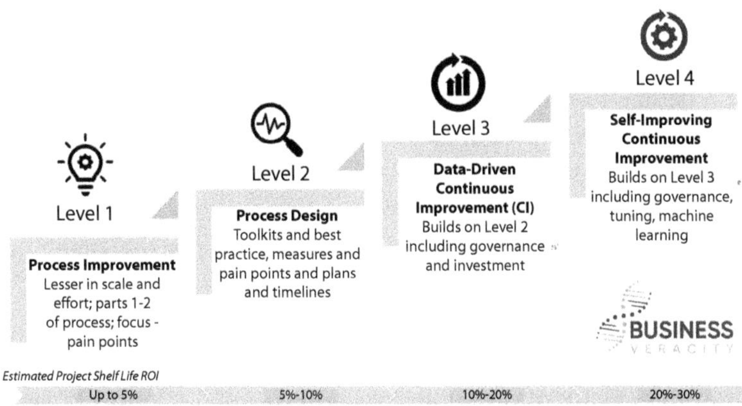

It may not sound like it, but this is more than a semantical difference or just corporate-term gold plating. Let's take a look at a couple examples of how we can put these ideas into motion.

Example 1: From Journey Map To Curated, Real-Time Experience Delivery

Process improvement initiatives such as constructing a set of customer personas and journey maps can be very impactful. Executing an initiative like that with a data-driven bias is even better, but I propose we move mature our process one more step and create a data-driven continuous improvement process.

- **Process Improvement:** A butcher paper journey map hanging on a board room wall directing our approach for a cohort of customer personas in a touchpoint or two. We are adjusting existing processes by adding some copy on the website and changing our marketing campaign touches to clarify specific product features.
- **Process Design:** The same butcher paper, but with a data discipline and methodology that truly captures accurate cohorts, their pain points, and accurately projects actions. We leverage that work to design specific experiences for segments or our customer base and have created a new set of processes. All this, holistically, but for a snapshot point in time.
- **Data-Driven Continuous Improvement (CI):** Expanding beyond design level and installing an overriding process that utilizes the data generated by a Customer's actual journey, where we personalize their experience and seamlessly apply intelligence gathered from their last N interactions with our Brand. CX leadership owns a governance process to hone over time.

Data points such as a single customer's tenure, communication preferences, service usage trends, website session data, or transcript elements from the last contact center agent or bot are contextualized against aggregate data models.

This allows us to turn that intelligence into bite-sized, next best actions defining what options our system offers the customer in digital channels and empowering our employees with relevant information.

- Self-Improving Continuous Improvement: The same CI solution above, but applying human governance, tuning, and machine learning to create a system that can improve the journey by enhancing its own models with the data it is capturing. When Customer elects to contact a live agent, we match that customer's specific needs to a specific employee's profile which is updated daily based on their performance outcomes.

Example 2: Better Bot Design: Using Analytics To Inform The Interaction Design Intelligently

Most people I know (other than people selling chatbots) hate chatbots. I know I do, as most bots are nothing but an unfilled promise of a better IVR.

Both voice IVRs and Chat Bots being examples of technology with tremendous promise, but in most implementations, the solutions leave the human interacting with the machine more frustrated than they were in the old fashioned, "press 2 for Spanish" IVR.

Armed with interactional data and our process design maturity models, we can anticipate how organizations at different levels of maturity may execute a virtual agent:

- **Process Improvement:** Call center costs are too high. Let's improve our cost by modifying customer service processes to deflect calls using a Chatbot.
- **Process Design:** After blowing up our existing IVR or bot, we use call center reporting to tirage the types of calls or times of day calls should be deflected to a chatbot.
- **Data-Driven Continuous Improvement (CI):** Constructing measures and supporting governance to detect friction points in the chatbot and human segmented interactions the tie to business outcomes. Investing in iterative improvements based on the findings.

At this maturity level, Increased Member Lifetime Value (MLV) comes into focus and deflection is no longer our Goal or KPI. Deflection is still measured as it is an element of the process.

MLV impact is measured by analyzing interaction data signals such as a Bot effectiveness KPI that is tuned against the MLV KPI.

Bot effectiveness measure constructed by indexing Ease and Resolution Signals which may look something like:

Ease Signal created by aggregating data such as:

✓ Repeated phrases during contact

✓ Count of bot intent fallbacks

✓ Contact duration between +/- 1 deviation of the mean

Resolution Signal created by aggregating data such as:

✓ Repeat assistance with similar contact drive in X hours

✓ Product or service session data related to contact driver

✓ Phrases used during interaction

- **Self-Improving Continuous Improvement:** A chatbot system that continually hones friction points in its interaction path by mining the terms used, applying machine learning, and continuously update the front end of that process regarding the language it's listening for and using. At this maturity level, the machine learning would be self-tuning against the MLV outcomes and the related Bot measures and signals.

Bottom line, in today's world of ever-increasing expectations and shorter shelf lives, winning companies are not just incrementally improving processes. They are investing in experience design united with mature data processes that are all but self-aware.

This approach creates systems that scales while adapting to our needs in the moment to empower our employees or wow our customers. As these systems get better at learning from their own interactions there will be little limit to the magical moments they can create for Brands.

About Daniel Dougherty

With more than 20 years' tenure leading customer experience organizations serving the world's top brands, Daniel Dougherty is an executive with a profound understanding of customer experiences and related employee behaviours.

Throughout his career, Daniel has created proven management systems, such as the Results Companies' CX360, which earned numerous industry honours including supporting clients' wins of J.D. Power awards for excellence in customer service.

Daniel is a Six Sigma Black Belt, CCXP, and certified COPC Customer Experience Implementation Leader who directs his own consulting practice helping organizations create value from technology, execute inventive operational approaches, and make decisions at lighting speed.

Contacts And Links

Email *Daniel@BusinessVeracity.com*

Website *www.businessveracity.com*

Linkedin *www.linkedin.com/in/danieljdougherty*

Twitter *www.twitter.com/DanielDougherty*

Facebook *www.facebook.com/WinningWithTech*

Fly Me To The Moon: Turning CX Dreams Into Reality

Olga Potaptseva

How to use agile CX management to achieve tangible CX improvements within three months.

Dear customer, please wait. Our great customer experience is under construction. A bunch of clever people supported by esteemed consultants are thinking through the strategy, your journeys, analysing the tons of feedback you have provided over the years and are trying to launch magnificent transformation projects. Just hang in there for a bit and in 2-3 years time your experience will be better than anywhere else. Whilst we are aspiring to be the Amazon of our industry please forgive us for poor customer service, reoccurring problems you have repeatedly told us about and lack of user experience across our channels. This is not for long! We value your business.

Yours faithfully, your favourite company.

Whilst building the foundations for customer experience is necessary and important, we must be fixing what is clearly broken now! Large-scale waterfall projects that deliver results in 2-3 years are not productive anymore, as the world around us is constantly changing. Using an agile approach to CX management instead is more effective in delivering long term goals. It allows breaking complex projects into small manageable chunks, learning fast and re-focusing effectively.

Big Projects Do Not Equate To Big Results

70% of all transformations fail, according to McKinsey research. Let us see why this may be.

If you and I decided to fly to the moon today, we would explore gravity first, then see what we know about the atmosphere, assess the materials and the tools we have available, and the people who have the expertise to support us. Then we would launch a small object or a robot onto the moon and explore its surface. Quite possibly we will experience setbacks, re-think our approach, and re-focus along the way. The magic rocket does not exist!

If you came to your leadership team suggesting that a CX Strategy, customer journey maps, educational masterclasses on the subject and a huge transformation plan would get them a perfect customer experience, what would be their reaction?

They might nod politely and ask you to try, but provide little support, scarce budget and mediocre engagement. Transformations are risky! Your career prospects will suffer. Even if the investment is limited to your salary, leaders would like to see your positive contribution to the business success.

According to TribeCX CEO David Hicks; of the CX practitioners who said their focus was to encourage their companies to make large investments in CX, only 51% had survived in their role beyond year 2. Of those who described their focus as building proof-points to establish the benefits from CX, 72% survived in their role beyond year 2.

You earn the right to ask for investment and resources only if you are able to demonstrate that CX focus delivers a real tangible benefit to customers and your organisation.

CX strategy, customer journey maps, robust measurements, customer centric culture are all essential to make CX a sustainable discipline in the long run. Take your time preparing, exploring the environment, building it brick by brick, whilst enhancing your reputation and buy-in for CX by delivering tangible improvements for customers now.

Identifying What Matters When You Just Don't Have Enough Evidence

So, if building the foundations, including voice of the customer programs, is a long-term game - how would you identify your critical projects?

In my role as a Head of Customer Experience for a UK bank I spent at least two days a week outside of my office. I sat with the contact centre agents, taking notes of repeat call reasons and exploring the supporting stats. I talked to the team handling complaints to see where we have the biggest volume and which ones are most prominent. I participated in process improvement initiatives to gain insights into where the employees struggle most. I have even spent at least a week with the Fraud Management department to establish their (and customers') pain points.

The questions I recommend you ask include:

- What are the internal sources of information you have at your fingertips?
- What customer problems do you hear about from your colleagues repeatedly?

Use your systems thinking and analytical abilities to identify a maximum of five projects that would make a difference to the customer experience. Bear in mind, these would need to be executed in the next three months so do take an effort to define them in a clear and actionable way.

Here is an example of how this approach works practically:

Using this approach, we recently started an initiative to "Reduce the proportion of contracts that take longer than 25 days to sign from start to finish from 15% to 9% by the end of quarter 2". We listened to our employees who told us that overly lengthy contracts cause a lot of stress, anxiety and bad memories for both customers and employees. As simple as that! As you see, we did not need a fully formed voice of the customer program to identify and fix what was broken.

Agile Execution To Turn CX Dreams Into Reality

I am sure you can now see how getting an approval for these small, tangible, low-risk, non-transformational and specific projects might be a much easier game. Obviously, you would have to do your homework and clearly demonstrate why these projects should be a priority. Things to consider may be reducing complaint volume, addressing operating costs, increasing propensity to buy, bringing down abandonment rate on the website, driving satisfaction rate up or other KPIs your organisation and leaders care about.

Now you have got the approval for the proposed projects. It is unlikely (and not advisable) that you would be the sole individual executing them, so the approval needs to include a firm commitment from the relevant functional heads. You would be looking for people who are already involved in the processes in question. The added bonus is that they were the ones pointing out the flaws to you in the first place!

With that in mind, team engagement should not be a problem.

However, the ability and habit to work cross-functionally towards the desirable customer outcomes is often not a strength for many organisations.

This is where agile execution comes in very handy. The first critical step in onboarding your new cross-functional team is to reduce anxiety. "I have a day job! How much extra effort is required from me?", "I think this is a big project. Am I now responsible for it?", "Is this another flavour of the month initiative?", "I've never collaborated cross-functionally before, and I am uncertain how this might work".

Using your emotional intelligence at this stage and addressing these concerns is key for success. Take the time to meet with people individually and in groups to explain how much time is required, what exactly they are expected to do, how you would be helping them, and what amazing results you are going to achieve for customers, colleagues, and the organisation together.

Agile CX implementation means clarity and that alleviates a lot of project start anxiety. With effective task setting, weekly scrums and bi-weekly retrospective meetings you teams will soon realise they are making progress fast and wasting little effort. They are focused, effective and efficient. They will grow to enjoy the rigour and the structure as it produces the benefits fast. And let us be honest, we all want to be part of successful projects. This sense of enjoyment will encourage your teams to participate in more CX improvement initiatives and engage others, thus building the cultural foundation for sustainable customer centricity.

There is no magic rocket that would deliver your organisation to the dream customer experience.

By rigorously focusing on the foundations, you are slowly building the infrastructure for sustainable customer centricity. Through the agile delivery of tangible improvements at the same time you are building the engagement and the culture for it. This approach will make you into a successful CX professional, improve your career prospects and get the much-needed buy-in from your leaders and colleagues.

Sources

- The 'how' of transformation, McKinsey Research 2016 https://www.mckinsey.com/industries/retail/our-insights/the-how-of-transformation
- How CX professionals can make themselves indispensable during tough times, Sampson Lee, 2020 https://www.mycustomer.com/customer-experience/loyalty/how-cx-professionals-can-make-themselves-indispensable-during-tough#:~:text=As%20TribeCX%20CEO%20David%20Hicks,their%20role%20beyond%20year%202.
- That's not how we do it here! John Kotter, Holger Rathgeber

About Olga Potaptseva

Olga Potaptseva is the Founding Director and CEO for the European Customer Consultancy that specialises in Agile CX Implementation. Her unique CX Implementation Toolkit allows clients across the world to launch and progress their CX efforts 3-4 times faster, by combining best practice in project management with deep expertise in customer experience. Olga is a strategic advisor to companies' C-Suites Executives and Leadership across multiple industry verticals and geographies, from the Middle East to the UK. Having started her career with GFK, one of the Top 5 market research companies, she realised that far too often valuable insights get shelved without generating a much-needed change. With her faith in real customer centricity, she sought a highly challenging position of the Customer Experience Head with one of the UK insurers. For six years, she relentlessly focused on driving customer centricity and succeeded in delivering business success through meeting customer needs. Since then, she held CX leadership positions in banking, telco and consulting.

Olga is passionate about promoting and advancing CX as a structured business discipline. She is an Executive Director for the Customer Institute, a regular Chair of Judges at customer experience awards, a founding member for the Women in CX community, a CXPA network lead, a keynote speaker and one of the Top25 CX Influencers of 2019.

Contacts And Links

olga@eucustomerconsultancy.com

www.eucustomerconsultancy.com

https://www.linkedin.com/in/olga-potaptseva

Creating Moments Worth Experiencing

Joanna Carr

Moments are perhaps the most sacred thing we have. In one single moment, you may smell the freshly brewed coffee, feel the hard pine wood as you rest your hands on your workspace, you may hear sounds of office chatter from colleagues or the stillness of your home office. In one moment, you can experience enjoyment, happiness, inspiration or contentment. Every moment is valuable; they make up our minutes, hours, days, and, ultimately, our lives.

Moments are unspecified time, compromising a bundle of multisensory experiences. Together these experiences transpire into emotions that become an impression (a story), that guides your employee/customer in their following action. Moments build on each other and over time, transpire to be a story worth living – or not.

This chapter delves into designing and achieving moments worth experiencing by taking a somewhat practical and holistic approach. Firstly, I will share a story from a brand that successfully delivers such moments throughout the entirety of their organisation, before introducing fascinating insights from Orlando Wood and his findings from the world of communication and advertising, where he offers fresh thinking about what businesses are missing in their approach to designing moments worth experiencing. The final part of this chapter offers practical tools to put your business into a position where it can deliver moments worth experiencing.

Turning Everyday Routines Into Meaningful Moments

I have had the great pleasure of working for two companies who live the story of moments worth experiencing. Two different industries, two different cultures – but one prevalent advantage, their advantage of fully understanding the value of every single moment.

For one of these companies, the focus on the moment is at the heart of their entire business, and you could say, is the essence of their business model. **Rituals,** international wellbeing and cosmetic company, have made it their mission to turn everyday routines into more meaningful moments. This mission can even be read on the walls inside their stores, but it's not what they say that makes these moments so significant - it's more about how they tell it, how they show it, definitively how they live it, and most importantly, how people feel it.

In my earlier role for Rituals, I once heard the CEO and founder, Raymond Cloosterman explain what makes Rituals so successful. Here, he talked about Rituals´ success not being down to one specific idea only, but all the thousands of small ideas and details that come together to make this happen. Understanding the importance of these small details and their part in the entire story's entirety is rooted in the leadership team and can be felt across the organisation.

If you have ever been into a Rituals store, anywhere in the world, you were most probably greeted by a smiling assistant, dressed in a smart oriental looking uniform, offering you a warm cup of tea. You may have experienced a treatment at the water island while chatting happily with one of the assistants, before leaving, probably a while later due to the mesmerising ambience. You may have learnt about stories from the east, received a gift and maybe personally been handed your bag from an assistant who came round from behind the counter.

While this is what a customer may be experiencing, so too are the employees. The attention to detail can be felt in their offices, meetings, training, product launches, and across their digital platforms.

Some Fresh Thinking That Could Benefit You

Rituals are not alone. Many brands and companies are succeeding at creating moments worth experiencing and are reaping the benefits such as being an attractive place to work, low sickness rates, low customer churn, high customer satisfaction rates, increased customer spend and ultimately differentiating themselves from the pack.

What you as a business leader or CX professional would like to know is: What are the successful businesses doing that is so unique? And more to the point, what can you do to create a working environment that can deliver moments worth experiencing across the entirety of your company?

Before answering these questions, I wish to shed some light on today´s situation. To do this, I'm going to borrow some intriguing findings from the world of communication and advertising.

Orlando Wood, the author of Lemon, has studied in-depth the effect of advertisement on emotions and the long-term effects. Wood has followed the changes within the world of advertisement, and business in general since 2006, and can show how there has been a definite decline in right-brain approaches to communication, meaning that we are both individually, but also on a societal and business level, slowly utilising less and less of the capabilities linked to areas such as empathising, seeing the whole picture, connecting with others, building relationships, self-awareness and context.

Instead, left-brain thinking is taking a more 'dominant role' with narrow thinking, categorising, factual, linear and repeatable action approaches.

What is truly interesting is that Wood´s research, informed by the ground-breaking work of neuropsychologist and psychiatrist, Iain McGilchrist, and his book; *The Master and His Emissary*, shows there is a significant difference regarding the effect on emotion and attention between right and left-brain approaches. Right-brain material engages considerably greater with emotional responses, increasing the attention span and creating a significantly longer-lasting effect than left-brain material, which delivers more short-lived responses.

In a conversation, Wood pointed out to me that: "It is essential to note that McGilchrist´s work referring to right-brain/left-brain differences is not based on the dated left/right-brained dichotomy in the 1970s, which suggested that the two halves of the brain do different things. McGilchrist´s work, however, teaches us that it's not that they **do different things**, but that they **do things differently**, bringing different attention types to bear on the world. They have different priorities and different takes on the world".

If we are to summarise these findings and use them to answer what successful companies such as Rituals are doing, we can recognise that they are not relying wholly on left-brain approaches within their communications and core business models, but instead combine the strategic and rational methods together with empathetical and creative approaches to evoke emotional engagement at a more profound and long-lasting level.

As to creating a working environment that can deliver moments worth experiencing across the entirety of your company, the answer lies in a very much underutilised area of work – an area typically given a left-brained approach, namely the implementation process of your company values. As Brene Brown shares from her vast experience of working within this field: "about 10 percent of organizations have operationalized their values into teachable and observable behaviours that are used to train their employees and hold them accountable."

Your company values, if implemented well, have the ability to create a waterfall effect throughout your business, generating a whole workforce operating together to create moments worth experiencing.

As a business leader you want to evoke emotional engagement and lasting attention; meaning that you must bring in some right-brain material and approaches, and not only rely on left-brained communication in the form of static material, such as written texts on your website, your employee handbook or the uncharming coffee cup or pen.

Practical Elements For Your Business Value Implementation Program:

1. Workshop for leaders where you map out key employee moments during a typical employee lifecycle. In such a workshop, you work with key moments to identify emotions you as a leader wish to evoke, using example questions found below.

The focus is on identifying what you wish the receiver to see, hear, feel and ultimately, experience within each moment, identifying which values and behaviours can support your work.

This mapping workshop should be amended and reproduced throughout all departments.

Mapping questions:

- What does ... (insert value) ... look like in this moment?
- What does ... (insert value) ... sound like in this moment?
- What does ... (insert value) ... feel like in this moment?

Moments in employee lifecycle	Interview	On-boarding training	Appraisal	Social activities	Meetings	Emplouee gifting	Employee farewell
Behaviour you wish to evoke							
Seeing							
Hearing							
Feeling							
Company value that may help you							
Your behaviour							

2. Encourage artistic means for living the values in everyday activities/moments. For example, when sending out a mandate for new project/activity to be done, assign a value that may challenge your employee to do the little extra. A small, yet powerful reminder like this, may encourage more conscious language use, improved aesthetic work or meeting environments, or even more thoughtful gift choices for your employees.

3. Exercises for new employees. For example, I have sent participants of onboarding training out to take creative photographs representing their values. The photos have been used to spark some fun guessing the photographed value for further reflection. This fun right-brained activity enhances the values memorability.

In addition, or alternatively, you may follow up with the mapping workshop.

Activities like these, create a room for discovery, questioning, experimentation and reflection; all attributes that encourage a design thinking mindset across your organisation.

Note: If these activities do not directly lend well to your organisation, try to translate them into something that can work for you. The point is, it needs to be an activity that creates engagement and memory.

4. Value story sharing. An example from this - A business I have been working with has implemented starting both team and formal meetings with a value story - recognising employees who deliver moments worth experiencing for either their colleagues or customers.

5. Create a film highlighting your values in action. This film may prove valuable for diverse situations such as job recruitment, onboarding or for sharing with customers and clients.

These are just a few suggestions from a CX designers toolbox, the important thing is that you evoke engagement and keep on doing it.

Tell It, Show It, Live It, Feel It

This chapter started with the angle that customers and employees' moments matter, not only to them but also to your business. Your ability to create an organisation that offers continuous and accumulative moments worth experiencing, will definitively determine whether customers and employees wish to continue being part of your story.

I have hoped to bring both awareness and inspiration towards making this an indispensable part of your CX design through a value implementation strategy, by seeing the value of combining both left-brain/right-brain approaches.

Going back to my earlier statement regarding Rituals, it's not what they say that makes these moments so significant - it's more about how they tell it, how they show it, definitively how they live it, and most importantly, how people feel it.

The real difference starts with you as a leader; you are the most significant brick in this design work, you have to tell it, show it, live it, and most importantly let your employees feel it.

Only then will it become real.

References

- Wood, O. (2019). Lemon, *How the Advertising Brain Turned Sour.* IPA
- Brown, B. (2018). *Dare to lead.* Vermillion, an imprint of Ebury Publishing

About Joanna Carr

Joanna Carr is a Customer Experience Consultant for Allegro, a technology and communication bureau based in Norway. Joanna is a founding member of the ECXO (European Customer Experience Organization), representing the Norwegian community space.

Originally from England, Joanna has worked within various customer-facing and head office roles for brands such as Estée Lauder, Bobbi Brown´s at Selfridges and later Rituals Scandinavia. Today, Joanna's areas of work includes: Customer experience strategising, service design, emotional intelligence in the workplace, Coaching, Customer service training and Speaking.

Contacts And Links

Links: *https://www.linkedin.com/in/joanna-carr-3a77b587/*
Instagram_ Joannacarrcx

Twitter: *https://twitter.com/joe290*

Website: *https://www.allegro.no*

Systems Thinking In Customer Experience Thinking

Edward Mei

Customer journey and user journey are often used interchangeably but really, they are two parts that make up the entire customer experience.

The customer journey deals with *behavior*. Emphasis is placed on encouraging customers to perform actions in a way that fits their needs. The user journey deals more with interaction. When customers are performing these actions, how the actions get accomplished and how the process is executed is at the forefront.

A system is a set of interconnected mechanisms and procedures that carry out a specific purpose. It takes inputs, performs a set of actions according to behaviors, and produces an output.

Together, the customer journey and user journey create a set of systems. A journey map, represented in this same way, is a system and each step of the journey is, in and of itself, a system. The design of systems drives customer experience.

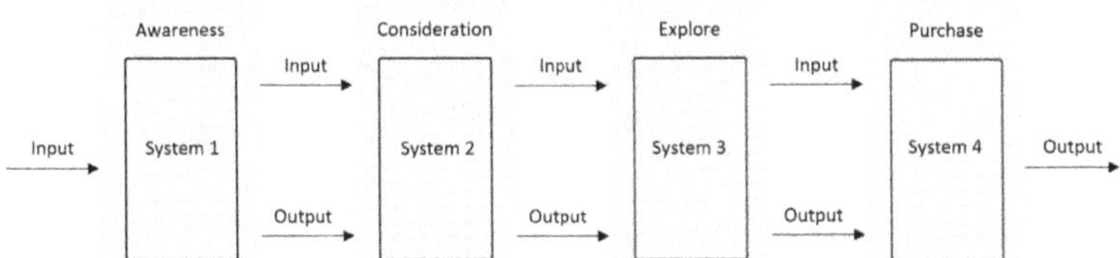

Systems Thinking in Customer Experience Thinking

Donella H. Meadows breaks down a system into three characteristics: resilience, hierarchy, and self-organizing.

Systems Thinking is an approach to understanding the interrelationships of individual parts in the context of their characteristics, patterns of behavior, and changes over time.

When building enterprise applications (hereinafter referred to as digital systems), we need to keep two kinds of customers in mind. The immediate customers are those that interact with and use the systems; they're typically internal employees and are regarded as end users. The extended customers are those of the company itself; they're entities and organizations who purchase products and services. All the information flowing through these systems is administered by its users but ultimately get extracted in various forms and delivered to the extended customers.

This chapter will primarily cover designing for the immediate customers, the end users. Their journey begins with getting requirements from their end customer, coming into the systems to enter information, performing sets of actions, and acquiring outputs. In all cases, a customer's journey includes the needs and requirements of extended customers which need to be considered

Resilience

The resilience of a system pertains to its ability to recover from or repair itself when affected by an outside force. Better yet, a resilient system has in place mechanisms to reduce the effects of unfavorable influences and behaviors, or eliminate them, as much as possible.

On subway staircases, there are often arrows on the steps to remind commuters to stay to the right. In buildings with lots of doors, there are signs that say "Enter" or "Exit" to ease the flow of foot traffic. Sinks have outlet holes that sit right below the top to prevent overflow.

An interesting aspect of working in a highly-regulated environment is data structures and customer deliverables have predefined rules. When designing and building a digital information system, the blueprint is already laid out; the types of data, its constraints, and its guidelines are preset. Sounds easy right? All we have to do is develop digital systems to follow these rules are we're golden – not quite. Guidelines are often vague and take expert knowledge to decipher. Other times rigidity inhibits users trying to get their work done. While they have to enter information, they also need to perform tasks and execute functions to manipulate that information. The challenge is one, getting users to enter information correctly and two, allowing them to use that information to complete their work without issues while rectifying errors along the way. Balancing both challenges takes a resilient system.

Designing for Resilience

The first challenge is met with human error; in this case it is unfavorable influence on our system. We start by placing our own restraints in the digital systems to ensure information is correct when it's first entered, rather than allowing users to enter the wrong information then notifying them later to fix it. In manufacturing, this concept is known as poka-yoke or 'mistake-proofing'. It prevents runaround and rework which puts a damper on the customer experience. The second challenge is handled by building flexibility into the system. Many times, incomplete information has to be entered first which becomes correct after the necessary manipulations are performed. We take into account whether the partial information is correct, even if it is incomplete, and then protect that information from erroneous manipulations. After all is said and done, the resulting data output must be correct.

Hierarchy

The hierarchy of a system has little to do with rank but more about the interconnectivity of system and its sub-systems.

In the example of resiliency, functions used to perform information manipulation are sub-systems of the digital systems as a whole. Larger systems can also connect with one another, which is an additional element of system hierarchy.

We can picture system hierarchy like this, where each circle is a system, and the inner circles are sub-systems:

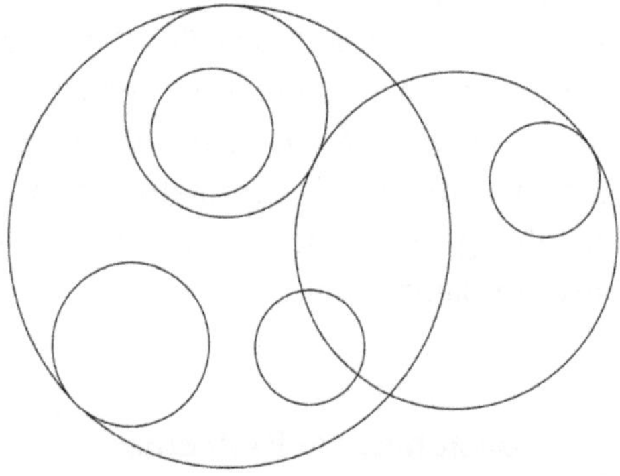

In the system of a restaurant, the kitchen and the table service are sub-systems. They are connected through the wait staff who takes customer orders, bring them to the back, then bring food to the table when it's ready. One way this system can be disrupted is if the restaurant is short staffed and someone from the kitchen needs to help wait on tables or if the host is busy and customers are kept waiting at the door.

In our digital systems, most functions are structured as workflows, much like steps depicted in a user journey map. The information entered into one process and is then manipulated. Data then flow, or is extracted, and is used in the next process. There are multiple sub-systems at play here so it could traverse multiple processes. Users from various departments across the organization interact with the information but only care about what they need. They have little knowledge of how the information got there or if it's correct for their specific work, yet they'll use it because the system provided it.

Designing to Include Hierarchy

Designing for hierarchy requires understanding the breakdown of systems, sub-systems, their interconnectivity, and how they relate. A key to this is different types of customers are interacting with the same systems. It's unrealistic to modify systems to account for the needs of distinct users and customers.

We tackle mosaic-like hierarchy and unique user needs by decoupling functions in our digital systems thoroughly. This adds additional touch points to ensure information is correct at each phase of the workflow. Information managed this way is also more easily understood. If users only want the information they need, they can get it from their step in the workflow or they can backtrack to see where it came from. Furthermore, each function can be run independently so users aren't forced to retrace multiple steps to generate a single subset of information. If the information a user wanted was produced by step four but it was connected with all previous steps, she would have to execute four functions to get the information, without seeing what's happening between each step.

Self-Organizing

A self-organizing system is one that can structure itself, create new structures, and complexify based on learning. A self-organizing system becomes more complex as it builds upon its resilience to prevent error or harm and expands the system hierarchy to optimize the interconnectedness of systems and sub-systems.

As systems self-organize, relationships between systems and

sub-systems evolve. Examples of self-organization can be most easily observed in nature, like how a chameleon changes its skin color to match its surroundings. In business, this equates to a "bottom-up" operating model where assets and decision-making powers are decentralized and influence starts with employees. In customer experience thinking, self-organizing systems empower customers to accomplish their goals with little friction and without interruption – a seamless experience.

In a hotel, the check-in/out process is automated with kiosks so customers can leave as they please without having to wait in line. Another upside, fewer employees need to be staffed at odd hours.

Designing a Self-Organizing System

A system becomes self-organizing through recognition of patterns – this is how it learns to create new structures and complexify. Most of the time, this requires human intervention. If customers are performing the same tasks at frequent intervals, make the tasks easier. If tasks are usually done in conjunction with other tasks, group them together to simplify the process.

1. Make sure not to break other parts of the system (resilience through decoupling)
2. Maintain communication within sub-systems and with other systems (managing flow through hierarchy). In this sense, self-organizing systems create more order and better structures.

In another sense, self-organization invites controlled chaos. Giving more autonomy in a decentralized fashion inevitably allows unfavorable behaviors; this is actually a blessing in disguise. Unfavorable behaviors to the system may be favorable to customers but the system can't handle them, yet another form of learning. This is the holy-grail of agile culture, a main tenant being autonomous and self-organizing teams. The teams are the customers, the agile methodology is the system, and the product is the outcome of their projects. Organizations with traditional structures are met with resistance and disruption when introduced to agile. It takes time for teams and organizations to learn to how to work in a new way. In time, agile transformation efforts create new processes and better structures, all the while growing more complex; it helps build better systems.

Bear in mind, when a system creates better structures through self-organization, users may abuse them. Metrics meant to monitor agile maturity can be skewed or even fabricated to give the illusion of progress. Many organizations give up on transformation efforts or settle for a half-baked approach because they can't overcome the chaos. Controls need to be in place to oversee customer behavior as the system continues to learn. Over time, these controls should regulate and adjust, rather than limit user action.

Lockheed Martin's Skunkworks is known for its highly experimental and cutting-edge projects. Founded in 1943, this group is fully autonomous but through guidance and support from the parent organization it continues to operate as a hub of innovation. One of the greatest inventions to come out of Skunkworks was America's first fighter jet, which was created in just 143 days. Google has an 80/20 policy where employees spend 80% of their time on core projects and 20% of their time on passion projects; Gmail was invented during that 20%.

Digital systems, in addition to direct contact with users and customers, can employ product telemetry tools to gauge user behavior. These tools collect data on how users act in the system to glean insights:

- Functions used infrequently are more difficult to navigate to make primary function screens less cluttered and easier to navigate.

- Functions used often are in the front and readily available.
- Functions that are important but used less frequently are in the forefront though out of the way so they can be executed as needed.

What users would love in a digital system is a blank screen filled with buttons, each with a precise function that generates the exact information they want. Sometimes it's still a wonder why we don't just do that, then we're reminded of the Hawaii false missile alert incident!

Focus On The System

The goal of many gym goers is to build muscles. There are plenty of ways to achieve that with lesser effort like taking Creatine or steroids or working out just to get a pump. The focus should be on practicing good form and building strength. Functional muscles will naturally grow as a bi-product of exercising correctly.

Our goal as customer experience leaders is to deliver remarkable customer experiences. Behind them are the systems that provide opportunities to facilitate these delightful experiences. We all start with the "why" – it's our purpose which drives us to create. Beyond that, the "how" is undoubtedly more important than the "what". Placing focus on what is being produced rather than how the system produces it results in a misrepresentation of its value. Cutting corners or masking inefficient system designs will hinder the possibilities of creating a truly enjoyable customer journey.

Systems designed with systems thinking concepts in mind complement all other aspects of customer experience. A focus on the systems does not diminish the importance of direct customer interaction; it makes those interactions more valuable since effort is spent on building relationships and further improving systems rather than correcting issues. Focusing on systems also helps place emphasis on metrics around growth instead of those aimed at minimizing failures. Well-crafted systems for customers mean more time evolving systems that promote a culture of behaviors empowering greater customer experiences down the road.

References

- Levy, J. (2015). UX Strategy: How to Devise Innovative Digital Products that People Love. Sebastopol, CA. O'Reilly Media, Inc.
- Meadows, D. H. (2008). Thinking in Systems: A Primer. White River Junction, VT. Chelsea Green Publishing.
- Senge, P. M. (2006). The Fifth Discipline: The Art & Practice of The Learning Organization. New York, NY. Doubleday.

About Edward Mei

Edward Mei is a product lead focused on building enterprise applications. As a certified scrum master and product manager, he specializes in product operations management and works with leadership across all levels to develop a product organization with agile maturity and customer-centricity.

Contacts And Links

Website: *https://edwardmei.me*

Email: *edwardmei92@gmail.com*

LinkedIn: *https://www.linkedin.com/in/edwardmei*

The Power of Recognition in CX Progress

Thomas Fairbairn

Recognition – the acknowledgment of people's best qualities - is a vital human need, and its critical importance has been understood throughout history: Cicero called it "not only the greatest of virtues, but the parent of all others." William Blake observed centuries later that "the thankful receiver bears a plentiful harvest", and it's in this context – the benefits that recognition can bring to everyone - that I'd like to discuss its importance in business and the customer experience you deliver.

Ideas that people have known for a long time (but haven't always appreciated enough) have been finding new life in the forward-thinking businesses of today. These are organisations that appreciate the advice of Jim Clemmer, who called recognition "the most inexpensive, easy-to-use motivational technique available to management." The more we understand customer experience, the more we realise that employees are the key to its success. And the more we understand employees, the more we realise that recognition is the key to theirs.

Recognition takes many forms, and there's not enough time in this brief chapter to outline them all. I will focus on two interrelated aspects of it: internal and external. Internal recognition is meaningful praise received within an organisation, from managers or colleagues, and the first part of the chapter will focus on that. The second half will outline the benefits of external recognition – the achievement of professional accolades such as awards – and how this can drive CX progress to new heights.

To start with, the significance of employees to the delivery of an overall experience is no longer in any doubt: a summary of various pieces of research showing how great employee experiences drive engagement, sales, customer loyalty (and more) can be found here.[1] This, of course, leads us to consider what exactly makes an employee engaged such that they facilitate great CX. Conventional factors such as pay and interest in their work are certainly important, but these factors depreciate in value significantly if there's no recognition behind them: after all, as Dr Bob Nelson has pointed out, "people may take a job for more money, but they often leave it for more recognition." This is borne out by industry research: a Deloitte study[2] found that companies with a strong internal recognition culture had 31% lower voluntary turnover amongst staff than those with a weak one. Typically, a strong internal recognition culture is defined not just by the presence – but the frequency – of praise for employee achievement. A study by Halo Recognition discovered that only 30% of employees are recognised more than once a year, but crucially also found that engagement rises by 35% if recognition is given daily.[3]

Whilst it's highly possible for employees to get survey fatigue, the same isn't true when it comes to praise. There isn't 'praise fatigue' in anything like the same way. The kinds of people that can get sick of praise are celebrities in the public eye: a worker at an organisation is quite likely, on the other hand, to feel undervalued and underpraised. Research from the American Psychological Association suggests only half of employees feel valued in their work.[4] There have been many steps to improve this in recent years, but the figure is still shockingly high when you think about it. Praise has to be specific: cookie-cutter praise is counterproductive, making the recipient feel generic and unseen for their own particular qualities, and can be worse than giving no praise at all. A Harvard Business Review survey found the words associated most with meaningful praise were "timely, relevant and sincere."[5] Companies that do the bare minimum to acknowledge their employees shouldn't be surprised when workers see right through it, and as long as some organisations treat their workers like expendable automatons, we shouldn't be surprised that one of the biggest sources of procrastination at work is employees looking for other jobs.

Recognition has a broader meaning once we look outside the four walls of an organisation – though its benefits are still keenly felt within. Of course, the most significant form of recognition for a company is the kind provided by its customers: the company should exist to delight them and provide a memorable experience. There are some great chapters in this book focusing on the precise ways an organisation can go about that. But the importance of recognition doesn't stop there. There are other external outlets for recognition, ones that can help a company figure out new ways of delighting their customers, and the most valuable form of this is entering awards.

There's an oft quoted saying from Henry Ford: "If I'd asked people what they wanted, they would have asked for faster horses." In bringing this up, I'm not trying to say that collecting feedback isn't necessary – it's absolutely crucial for delivering great CX – but the point here is that it's vitally important to look beyond your specific industry or sector in order to pick up new ideas. There are things that would delight your customers that they haven't told you about – simply because they've never been exposed to them. By exposing your organisation to the rigours of a cross-sector awards programme, especially one like the International Customer Experience Awards that lets you see other companies' presentations, you'll be able to hear from a wide range of companies and broaden your horizons. Some of these ideas might not have occurred to you – or your customers!

External recognition is also a great way of boosting team morale and connecting your organisation's work into the wider

CX movement. The entry process itself is beneficial for the team: they have to explain their initiative from first principles, and the need to do this in a clear, concise way tends to crystallise their understanding and appreciation of the work they've been doing. Then there's the boost to morale that comes from victory. Internal recognition schemes can be organised in an engaging and enjoyable way, but by their nature (being internal), they won't be able to match the excitement and stakes of an external ceremony.

One of Oracle's Cloud Transformation Directors, Emma Sutton, explained this importance when describing the UK Customer Experience Awards, calling it "a fabulous experience, with so many CX professionals in one place. How could one leave without feeling even more motivated about putting customers at the heart of your business?" Harvard Business Review's research echoes this point, saying that employees need a blend of regular recognition and other forms of recognition that occur a few times a year: awards are a key part of that long-term recognition process. As they put it, employees consider these "important milestones that provide clues about their progress and performance. When a manager skips them, employees often infer that they, not the procedure, are what the manager doesn't value."

This point about milestones is very significant. The best CX awards programmes offer feedback reports with comments from an expert judging panel, and this feedback can be crucial when it comes to improving CX strategy. Advice here is pitched at the managerial level, rewarding leaders for going beyond their company silo and sharing their story with a wider audience by giving them actionable insights. It's only by taking that leap that you can get the final benefit of outside recognition: publicity for your organisation. This can be an internal benefit, such as meeting a like-minded professional at the event and forming a connection, but also external. Receiving an award from a respected organiser can form part of your marketing strategy, and victory in CX awards in particular is a way of showing your customers that you take your CX journey very seriously.

I think this is crucial advice for managers, especially ones that unconsciously allow their own standards of recognition to become the norm across their organisations. A small group of people like to claim they don't need recognition, perhaps because they think they sound impressive or self-sufficient. I don't agree. Confucius may have said that "the superior man… is not distressed by the fact that men do not recognize the ability he has", but it was easy for him to say that when followed by disciples who hung on his every word! People making this claim might think they've achieved enough recognition for what they do, but this can blind them to the fact that it's still very important for others – and themselves.

The research presented in this chapter shows that recognition is of vital importance to an ordinary employee: organisations therefore need to acknowledge its prominence in their day-to-day operations. This means adopting a blend of internal and external recognition schemes, ranging from specific praise on a daily basis all the way up to participating in awards programmes that take place every year. Employees need to feel part of something special on many levels: within their team, within their company, and within the wider business landscape. Companies that appreciate this will be able to increase their employee engagement, and in turn, empower their staff to deliver an unforgettable customer experience.

References

1. "10 stats that show the undeniable connection between EX and CX": https://www.ringcentral.co.uk/gb/en/blog/10-stats-that-show-the-undeniable-connection-between-ex-and-cx/

2. "Becoming irresistible: A new model for employee engagement": https://www2.deloitte.com/us/en/insights/deloitte-review/issue-16/employee-engagement-strategies.html

3. "Top 5 Employee Recognition Initiatives": https://halorecognition.com/wp-content/uploads/2019/03/HALO-Top-5-Employee-Recognition-Initiatives_Final-2019-1.pdf

4. "APA Survey Finds Feeling Valued at Work Linked to Wellbeing and Performance": https://www.apa.org/news/press/releases/2012/03/well-being

5. "The Little Things That Make Employees Feel Appreciated": https://hbr.org/2020/01/the-little-things-that-make-employees-feel-appreciated

About Thomas Fairbairn

Thomas Fairbairn is Business Writer at Awards International. His work focuses on synthesising the lessons from the Awards International community and beyond, providing useful advice that helps companies realise their potential and gain recognition for their inspiring efforts. With a background in theatre and experience in writing for wide audiences, he brings a unique perspective to debates around customer and employee experience.

Contacts And Links

thomas@awardsinternational.com

www.awardsinternational.com

https://www.linkedin.com/in/tom-fairbairn-a9a984180/

5. CX Metrics, Measurement And ROI

Using feedback and metrics to better understand commercial results

Are You Listening To the Whole Picture?

Nick Lygo-Baker

What is a Customer Experience? There are many explanations, but I thought I would share how I describe this to others when talking about CX. Dangerous territory I know, given this chapter is nestled in a book of highly respected experts on this very topic!!

"Customer Experience (CX) is a dynamic combination of conscious and subconscious emotions, resulting in the perception a person has about an organisation or brand. The influences that an organisation, it's people, it's products, and it's digital technology has on every touch-point that a person experiences, triggering memories over time."

Great – so what? Sounds both fluffy and yet still technical? But, how can we use this understanding to our advantage?

This is where Experience Management comes into play. By understanding what triggers a memory about an experience, the more control we can have in repeating this and therefore, we can create intentional future positive customer outcomes.

Designing the experience deliberately and with purpose, organisations can seek to manage the consistency of the delivery of their customer's experience.

Sounds easy enough, but why do so many companies get this so badly wrong? How can organisations move away from creating great customer experiences by accident based on the skills of individual staff, to having a high degree of intentional service delivery which, consistently meets customer needs and expectations?

There are so many important touchpoints that are involved in creating a customer experience in the best way. Meeting these expectations and providing the ideal customer outcome requires people in the business to have awareness of these insights and then act with purpose.

The importance of measuring the touchpoints in a way that feeds back to those conscious and subconscious emotions cannot be underestimated. This helps organisations address customer needs and expectations at a base level.

Organisations by default have the desire to track and trend everything as a number, a metric which can be used to evaluate performance good or bad! The irony of CX is that it is an emotional human response to an experience. Creating a metric around something that can be intangible is a challenge. As a result, there is no one metric that can provide the whole truth about customer experience.

"Not all people experience the same event in the same way."

There are Five Voices of CX measurement which should be used in combination to get a truly rounded, holistic picture of how an organisation is performing. Often referred to as a Listening Post, hearing each aspect of the business and drawing meaningful insights by integrating these performance measures, will provide a robust foundation for decision making and understanding actual performance.

The Five Voices are:

Quite often businesses will deploy two or three of these measures with the focus being on the voice of process! Typically, business measures are used as Key Performance Indicators (KPI's). These are used to set targets and incentivise employees to deliver them. This isolated method can miss the point entirely, and whilst logical, chasing a score can be a dangerous practice. This drives the wrong behaviours, promotes decisions that are not in the interest of the customer, employees and ultimately the organisation.

However, if the focus is on the customer outcome, aligning these five measurements and combining them gives a more balanced set of insights, providing organisations with the levers required to optimise performance:

#1 Voice of Customer (VoC)

VoC is about listening to what customers have to say via surveys, their actions, habits, and complaints. Capturing this voice is vital to understand the customer who ultimately pays the bills. This can be split into two types of listening posts: Transactional and Relational. They measure a single transaction and the overall relationship but are limited is used in isolation.

Transactional feedback is more commonly collected as complaints as well as satisfaction surveys that are deployed at any point during a transaction journey. Most surveys happen after an engagement or touchpoint such as a purchase or speaking with a contact centre agent. The purpose of the survey is to collect and understand the engagement from the eyes of the customer.

There are a variety of survey methods for collecting feedback. The best practice is to reflect the channel the customer chose to make contact through, this can be online, by phone, SMS, video, social-media, or face-to-face.

Each channel has a "research factor" impacting the consistency of the output, making it hard to combine data sets. A human response will be influenced based on the channel by which they have been engaged. For example, the written word will be different to a voice or video response. People tend to give positive feedback the more considered they are about their experience.

Getting as close as possible to the "moment of truth" means you can get more emotion and rawness from the narrative in the feedback.

Knowing how to interpret these insights is critical. Misreading data in decision making can be disastrous. This can be caused by incorrect questions or limiting pre-coded answers. When it comes to conducting correlative analysis there will be an impact on the outcomes and validation.

"Bad Data In = Bad Data Out" *

Layer the question inaccuracy with the incentivisation of respondents to complete a survey by using prize draws, plus targeting staff on scores, and your data quality is ruined. The importance of avoiding such practices where possible cannot be understated.

#2 Voice of Employee (VoE)

Now I don't mean the traditional annual surveys that ask whether you like your benefits package, or if you get paid enough? We all know the answer to those questions. What I mean here by Voice of the Employee is different; Are employees experiencing the customer journey in the same way as customers? Voice of Customer through Employees (VoCE) if you like, where surveys and measures for VoC and VoCE are applied in parallel to see if there is an experience expectation gap. Those Employees closest to the customer touchpoint will have valuable knowledge on any failing or if process change is required.

Only 41% of employees** feel strongly that they know and understand what their company stood for and why that made them different from the competition.

Truly engaging employees is important. They must understand the business purpose and company vision, so they then know what the business expects them to deliver to customers. A lack of engagement here will have a direct impact on loyalty and sense of purpose for employees and how they carry it forward to customers.

Companies need to be open with employees from the start. Feedback mechanisms can be met with a degree of cynicism. As such, the nature of the feedback will be positively biased, as people fear they will be identified and punished. Organisations must embrace feedback; show they are listening and then act upon it, to demonstrate they are taking their employees seriously. This will reveal knowledge and recommendations that can solve issues leaders may not even know exist.

#3 Voice of Service (VoS)

VoS is measured by mystery shopping or compliance audits to understand the effectiveness of training and how this translates through employees to customers. By mirroring genuine customer personas in the recruitment of mystery shoppers, researchers replicate genuine scenarios that measure service delivery across the core customer journeys.

There are two main approaches to Mystery Shopping. A large panel of profiled "genuine customers" who can provide a consistent measurement of service delivery, or secondly a small panel of trained auditors who can provide more detailed process checks. Both are valid depending on questions they are looking to answer.

The point here is to ensure that there is a measurement which monitors the consistency of service delivery whether B2C or B2B. How staff training translates to the shop-floor customer experience. Often this is the missing insight between Customer and Employee measures and why there can be a disparity in the findings. Measurement should follow a common theme, by seeking to understand the impact on a customer, not to create a score employees are targeted against.

Using the premise of "what gets measured gets done" *** visibility and a prioritised level of importance will be given the focus. Therefore, if the focus is to get a high score, this will be the driving factor and not the experience of the customer. Whilst the two may be aligned, this will be more by accident than intentionally. The core elements that impact a customer's experience will be overlooked and the organisation will be off target – ironically!

Historically, Mystery Shopping was used a stick to beat staff with but is now an extremely valuable means of "catching" people doing the right thing! Rewarding behaviour and publicly praising staff shows other colleagues what good looks like and reassures customers.

#4 Voice of Process (VoP)

All organisations create processes, from supply chains and people policies to technology and digital interfaces etc... These processes become Key Performance Indicators (KPIs) used for performance measurement. However, process measurement should not be designed with the KPI's intended as the end outcome. Businesses who do this, are likely to discover something wrong when a customer complains. Given only 4% of customers affected are likely to complain – this can have a long-term impact on both immediate performance and long-term customer loyalty.

Organisations will have business analysts looking at

performance of their process, uptime, and efficiencies. This can be used to both forecasting stock supplies or service outages and identify at which point the customer will feel the impact of such issues along their journey. Businesses have service level agreements (SLA) with their suppliers in order to ensure they are able to meet forecasted sales – however, if this was based on meeting customer needs would this change the urgency or increase the SLA's?

Prior notice provides the window of opportunity, not only to inform a customer of an impending issue, but to act and to rectify the issue before it has a wider impact on the customer. This is not a metric that organisations connect with customer experience. After all this is an internal process measurement? Right?

The point is that all business processes directly or indirectly impact the customer outcome in some way. Whether this is a Head Office finance clerk processing a supplier payment or a waiter serving in the restaurant, everyone in an organisation has a role to play in delivering to the customer. This should be the purpose of the business process measurement.

#5 Voice of Market (VoM)

Understanding the direction and trends in your market and parallel markets can be just as important as listening to your current customer base. Where is the share of mind as well as share of wallet coming from? Will you remain in the evoke set for decision making, or are you at risk from competitors in your market or new emerging markets?

Businesses need to know who their audience is, together with how tolerant their brand equity is before customers seek alternative solutions. This may not always be obvious. For example, smartphones have replaced, compact cameras and MP3 music players, absorbing their capabilities into one device. The market has evolved, and two of these products have become obsolete.

Organisations need to measure the share of mind and share of wallet. What do customers buy from you, what combinations of products and services are bought and what are their alternatives? By developing an understanding of the customer needs organisations can identify the way in which they can leverage digital technology, service changes and combining solutions to provide greater customer enrichment to maintain relevance in the market.

Measure the wrong thing or measure in the wrong way, and you may be making decisions on duff data which is more dangerous than not measuring at all!

Mixing The Beat

All good measurement starts by mapping how the customer experience, employee experience and business is performing in every aspect in the present. Conducting a maturity assessment will determine the readiness of an organisation to adopt change before mapping the desired future state. Perform the gap analysis, identify the priorities, and then measure, measure and measure again the impact of change. Too few organisations start with this basic CX principle.

As you will have gleaned from this chapter, the way in which measurement is applied needs to be considered and thought-out, plus given the same purposeful approach as any other foundational business activity.

One key business challenge is that different functions within organisations can often build measurements for their own purpose, without consideration of wider opportunities to integrate data points and incorporate more holistic insight needs.

This disparate approach can hugely increase the overall cost, by running similar measurement processes designed to perform only one function. This fails the business, wasting money and seeing much more limited return on CX investments.

Thriving organisations were conceived or have adapted to work much more collaboratively and measure the right things in the right way. These measures must start by:

1. Identifying the right listening posts for the business
2. Connect the right channels to reach the entire audience and beyond
3. Collaboration, designed with purpose to ensure maximum return

By collaborating on the measurement process, organisations can design them to work cost efficiently together, providing deep and meaningful insights that point to actions that will improve customer experience, employee experience and business performance!

References

- * Fuechsel G. – (1900's) Adapted from "Garbage in, Garbage out concept in computer science
- ** Fleming J.H. and Whitters D. (2012) Gallup Business Journal.
- *** Drucker P. (1954) Adapted from "The practice of Management" Harper & Row – New York

About Nick Lygo-Baker

Nick is a leading expert in operationalizing customer insight and customer strategy and was listed in the top 25 CX influencers listed by CX Magazine and top 150 Global Influencers and Thought Leaders by SurveySensum. As both a Certified Customer Experience Professional and a Certified Member of the Market Research Society, Nick has been helping brands measure and improve their customer experience for almost 20 years.

He has held global leadership roles within some of the worlds' top Customer Research organisations. Nick founded Paradigm CX Ltd in 2018, providing a virtual-CXO solution with hands on guidance for organisations looking to improve their Customer Experience.

A millennial Retail graduate, Nick's experience covers a broad range of B2C and B2B industries (including Retail, Hospitality, Financial Services, Pharma, Automotive and Public Sector) designing some of the most innovative and engaging Voice of Customer, Mystery Shopping and Employee Feedback Solutions.

Contacts And Links

LinkedIn: *https://www.linkedin.com/in/nicklygobaker*

LinkedIn: *https://www.linkedin.com/company/paradigmcx*

Instagram: *https://www.instagram.com/paradigmcxltd*

Twitter: *https://twitter.com/CXParadigm*

Facebook: *https://www.facebook.com/ParadigmCXLtd*

Website: *https://www.paradigmcx.com*

Drive Value Or Find Yourself A New Job!

Olivier Mourrieras

Tracking return on customer experience investment is a competency that has finally matured across the CX community. With priorities a lot more fluid and investment choices harder to make, CX practitioners need to respond by enhancing the visibility of their value delivery, and they need to do so in near real time. This chapter contains proven practices that will help you ensure customer experience remains considered as one of the top value drivers in your business.

Recognise The Reality Of Shortening Business Cycles And Narrowing Executive Bandwidth

Business cycles have been getting shorter and shorter and the global pandemic has certainly further accelerated that trend. It will not slow down. The upcoming rebound will give way to a new type of similarly fast paced, although perhaps more predictable cadence. Businesses face tremendous fluctuations in cash flow, available resources, demand levels, and radically changing customer needs.

In my time as a customer experience leader, up to the end of 2017, I recall committing to boards and committees on actions and projects spanning well over six months, even a year. Six months or a year to deliver a project just seems inappropriate now. I realized the full extent of the change in the time horizon of projects when recently supporting a not-for-profit housing association in their transformation journey. The executive sponsor of the work we were supporting there said to me, "Olivier, three month sprints don't stand a chance anymore, we need to slice the bigger problems in chunks we can fix in ten to 30 days and double down on the financials".

This was in June 2020.

The intellectual capacity executives can allocate to individual topics keeps shrinking with too many decisions competing for immediate attention. CEOs are expected to ensure they meet the needs of all their stakeholders, delivering on environmental, societal, regulatory, ethical, social, and many more matters. They pass on that pressure to their executive teams.

It is important that you as CX practitioners understand this context and how it translates to your business so that you are able to navigate this new world and get the most out of it for your customers.

The Solution Part 1: Show Me The Money

There are many reasons for this, for example:

- Low sample numbers result in weak confidence levels
- Events such as an advertising campaign by a competitor, a new regulation or any external factor within the industry which affects customers' decision making processes
- Extraordinary environmental and societal factors

The most successful companies steer their CX investment decisions by combining as many meaningful metrics and indicators as possible to demonstrate the patterns of customer and business impact related to an activity.

Compiling an holistic audit of all metrics available, to find those that are relevant to value in the specific case you want to put forward, will help enrich the mix. All metrics should be considered such as:

Strategic NPS	Lead time	Internal attrition
Journey/transaction NPS	Channel mix	Churn
Effort score	Social media engagement	Bad debt
Cost per call/ interaction	Repeat calls	14-day cancelations
Number of handoffs	Hacks	Renewal rates
First call resolution rates	Compliance (process and journey)	Returning customers
Frequency of contact	Defect rates	Referrals
Click rates & Conversion rates	Rejection rates	Cancelled appointments by field engineers
Views	Complaints	CO2 emissions
Wish list additions	Penalties	Resource consumption
Basket additions	Number of colleagues involved	etc.
Additions conversion	Colleague engagement scores	

This is most successful when the list of potential drivers is co-created with key business partners, identifying the 'low hanging fruit' that can be measured and prioritised for the specific case in the given time window. This will also help comprehension of the issues and aid stakeholder buy-in.

The Solution Part 2: Appeal To The Emotions And Deliver On The Brilliant Basics

Companies delivering market leading loyalty are increasingly turning to in-depth customer interviews to help build patterns and model likely outcomes. This allows them to move forward with pace and confidence when there are too few data points for a quantitative analysis. Some schools of thought defend the fact that patterns should start to appear from nine data points.

Demonstrating that the initiative you are proposing has the approval of customers saves time. Using customer verbatim and video testimonials is a powerful way to appeal to the emotions of your leadership team. They are increasingly being accepted as early proof points that allow projects to move to the next phase where more robust data can be collected.

In times of uncertainty, focus on efficiency gains and consistent delivery of the core elements of your service. For example, consistently reducing the time each interaction takes will save cost and customer irritation. Few industries have short enough repeat purchase cycles to demonstrate retention gains. Rather, demonstrate the reduction of delivery and waiting times, number of touchpoints, improving timeliness, first time completion, reducing your channel mix and the number of times the customer needs to switch channels. Improve these and retention will improve!

Leading businesses increasingly prioritize activities that minimise their business' exposure to negative reputational risk. CX leaders in these companies understand how an initiative, product or service will help neutralise risk and guarantee the company's future viability and success. The time when early global pandemic errors were tolerated is long gone. Customers' zero level of tolerance has (regrettably) propelled risk management to become one of the top three board priorities.

The Solution Part 3: Keep It Simple And Make It Easy For The Leadership To Agree To Your Request

You are now equipped with a compelling proposal and evidence that SOME value will be generated from your initiative. You now have prioritization, lobbying and packaging work to do to gain the support of your key executives. But remember that their intellectual bandwidth has shrunk.

Successful change leaders such as yourself, continuously use a stakeholder map, much like the one you would use in the redesign of a customer experience. They just use the tool internally and dynamically to stay relevant. Because you have very little time to sell your case, you need to make sure you stay on point, that you continually understand, influence and leverage the dynamics in your stakeholder map. It is not a one-shot action; it is a daily routine. This is where I have made mistakes a couple of times before: you drop the ball for just a few weeks and your programme is off the chart for the next six months and you will need to expend considerable energy to get it back on track.

Once you understand your stakeholder map, make sure you are aligned:

- Aligned with the company vision, purpose and brand promise
- Aligned with key executives' and corporate objectives
- Contributing to the big issue of the moment
- Thinking holistically: even if your customer sentiment is the best proxy for measuring long term business success, executives will still expect evidence of short-term commercial value for their other stakeholders.

On the big issue of the moment, if you know some consultants are hanging around the corridors, figure out what they are trying to sell and what reception it is getting. This might help you get ahead of the curve.

Conclusion

So, with timescales changing, you, as a CX practitioner, need to become more creative and invent a new and richer mix of value drivers, backed up with factual evidence. With the number and hierarchy of topics shifting at the executive table, it is also time to be a lot more focused and self-aware of your own relevance. Combining these evolving skills and competencies, you can continue to give customer experience (and yourself) the place it deserves on the corporate agenda.

Now, you might think this chapter has a rather short-term view of the topic and I agree. In fact, it is meant to provide ideas and tips to respond to the challenge now, so that you don't have to update your CV just yet! Customer experience is a long-term game but now, more than ever, customer experience leaders and change agents must succeed in the short term, while investing for the long term. As David M. Cote writes in his book *Winning Now, Winning Later*, "We need to push ourselves to achieve seemingly conflicting things at the same time — short term performance and investment in the future."

About Olivier Mourrieras

Olivier Mourrieras is a management consultant, coach, speaker and board advisor who has led large scale and leading edge customer experience transformation plans at Orange Business Services and E.ON from 2005 to 2017.

He founded his own consulting company CX-Impact in 2017. He is also Board Advisor for TribeCX and trainer for This is Service Design Doing. He shares his passion for customer experience and enriching the lives of customers with his clients.

Olivier provides personalized advice and coaching support for leaders and companies aiming to embed a customer centric culture, innovate and improve their customer experience.

His background in customer operations brings a very practical and energizing touch to his approach and in particular how to define customer centric visions, translate them in customer impact, target improvement areas and upgrade the customer centric corporate agenda to enable the front line sustainably.

Contacts And Links

olivier.mourrieras@cx-impact.com

https://cx-impact.com

www.linkedin.com/in/oliviermourrieras

Setting Up A Voice Of The Customer (VoC) Program From Scratch

Gabriela Geeson

What is a voice of the customer program? It is simply having a framework in place that is going to help your organisation understand their customer experience (CX). It is about having a formalised way to collect and analyse customer feedback and have some metrics in place that can help establish a baseline and measure the customer experience. One of the main benefits is that you can monitor any changes in customers' perception over time and even predict their behaviour.

A VOC programme should encompass the following four key elements:

1. **Listen and capture feedback:** so that we can understand some of these questions: What is the customer journey? What customers like and dislike about the service and how can we improve their experience?
2. **Analyse and measure trends:** are there any trends, changes in perception over time or after a change has been implemented? How is each area/market performing? What are the opportunities for improvement? How customer satisfaction impacts conversion/retention and ultimately revenue?
3. **Distribute insights to key stakeholders:** this can be done in different ways depending on what your stakeholders will find

useful, for example your executive team might want to see monthly summaries/reports but heads of departments might want to access a dashboard weekly.

4. **Act on results:** from coaching, improving processes, to different product and marketing initiatives. It is great to capture customer feedback, but you need to act on it.

There are also tools out there that can make it easier to summarise, visualise and share insights as well as monitor results in real time, but they can be costly so depending on the size of your business you might want to start with creating and sharing reports in a simple format. Once your program is mature, you can put a case together to implement the right technology/ tools to showcase all insights.

How To Build A Program From Scratch?

Depending on the size and maturity of the business, there might be some sort of customer feedback that is already collected so the best thing to do when starting a new program is to understand what is available and how it is used.

Assess whether there are any customer experience metrics in place and whether they are being used and how. A critical part of this assessment is to establish whether or not the right methodology is being used to measure customer experience. For example, I've come across businesses that are using Net Promoter Score (NPS) as their CX metric but aren't using the right scale or asking the standard NPS question. Any deviation from the original methodology is going to have an impact on the results and it will leave you with an inaccurate score.

Once you've done your assessment you can start drafting a plan. A plan should include a high-level overview of your customer journey so that you can identify the moments in the experience that need to be measured. For example, some key moments on the customer journey could be when customers download an app, register as a customer, after an interaction with a customer support agent or when receiving a product or service.

Stakeholder engagement is also an important element of setting up a program. It's essential to have conversations with your internal stakeholders to understand their view and experience of the different metrics. This information will be useful when making final recommendations. The metrics should be agreed with your executive team and ideally there should be an executive sponsor. Depending on their experience with different metrics they might have an opinion and/or preference. I sometimes think of NPS as one of our British brands 'Marmite'; it is a spread that people tend to have on a slice of toast, some people absolutely love the flavour and some people absolutely hate it. In the same way some people love and others hate NPS and although it might not seem important, it will determine your stakeholders' engagement with the program so it is crucial that they believe in the metrics that the company is going to adopt. At the end of the day, what is important is to adopt a metric that can help to measure and improve the experience, regardless of whether it is Net Promoter Score or Customer Effort score or any other metric.

Different companies take different approaches, but it is good practice not to rely on just one metric. Having more than one metric helps you to sense check and gives you a wider perspective. When selecting a metric, my experience has been that people find it easier to follow one score but that doesn't mean you can't use more than one metric. You can have a primary metric, for example Customer Satisfaction Score (CSAT), which can be measured at the different levels from the touch point level up to the brand level but you can also include NPS in some of your surveys. Both metrics should work hand in hand, but the spotlight will be on your primary metric.

Customer Experience Metrics

These are the most commonly used metrics:

Customer Effort Score (CES) is a metric designed to measure the ease of an experience. It asks customers to rate the ease of using products or services on a scale of 'very difficult' to 'very easy'. Here is the formula that is used to calculate this:

CES score (%) = (sum of all responses/
total number of responses) x 100

Customer Satisfaction Score (CSAT)

It indicates how satisfied a customer is with a specific product, transaction, or interaction with a brand and you can calculate it as follows:

CSAT Score (%) = (Number of Extremely Satisfied
+ Satisfied responses)/ (Total number of responses) x 100

Net Promoter Score (NPS)

It measures the likelihood of your customer recommending your service or product to friends or colleagues by using the following question: On a scale from 0-10, how likely are you to recommend us to a friend or colleague?

To calculate your Net Promoter Score, subtract the percentage of Detractors from the percentage of Promoters for example if 60% of respondents were Promoters and 10% were Detractors, your Net Promoter is a score of 50.

According to Bain & Co, the creators of NPS, any NPS score above 0 is good, meaning that your audience is more loyal. Anything above 20 is considered good, above 50 is excellent, and above 80 is world class.

Internal Communications

Once again, we need to think about our stakeholders and what would be the best way to share all your VOC insights with them. With that in mind, create a list of all your stakeholders and next to each stakeholder add the channel and format you're going to use to communicate with them. This will be your communications plan and to be effective, a two-way communication should be encouraged. The success of the program depends on how actionable and useful the insights are, so we need to make it easier for our stakeholders to understand and act on customer feedback.

It is important to have a holistic view of your customer experience and you can achieve that by not just looking at solicited feedback but by combining your operational data with your solicited and unsolicited feedback; for example the number of customers who use your service every month, the number of customers who churn every month and combine that with the feedback you've received and collected. This approach will enable you to see the 'WHAT', which are the customer behaviours when your customers interact with your brand and the 'WHY' behind that behaviour.

Operational Data examples (WHAT)	Customer Initiated Feedback examples (WHY)	Initiated by your organisation feedback examples (WHY)
Funnel drop off analysis	Customer contacts (email, chat, etc.)	NPS, CSAT, CES surveys
New customers	IVR (voice feedback)	Customer research
Live time value	Social media platforms	User research/Usability & Product testing
Number of transactions	Reviews sites	
Call, chat, mail volumes		
First call resolution		
Wait time		
Web and App up time		
Web and App load time		

There should be a healthy balance between the internal and external view of the customer. Most businesses have a lot of operational data but very little experience data; that's why it is important as Customer Experience professionals to help businesses to achieve that balance.

Another source of truth that should help you to assess the status of your customer experience is the 'Voice of the Employee', because if employees are engaged/satisfied or disengaged/dissatisfied, it will have a very big impact on the customer experience.

Governance

It is important to have good governance from the beginning of the program so that it is clear how the program will be managed and how the insights will be shared with the different stakeholders and how you are going to act on this or close the loop.

Closing the loop is about taking practical steps to act on customer feedback and respond to them in the best possible way so that they know you're taking their feedback seriously and using it to improve the experience with your service or product.

An example of this could be contacting a customer who provided a negative review or raised an issue. Also, analysing trends to determine root cause and as a result of this create new processes, improve features or an area of the experience that isn't working very well.

When you have a large customer base, there are tools that can help you automate some processes to close the loop. Some businesses set different strategies for the different groups depending on their rating, for example different strategies for promoters or detractors, satisfied or dissatisfied. In addition to, or as an alternative, you can create themes with the insights collected and use those to identify opportunities for continuous improvement. And once some initiatives are underway, you can give customers an update on progress; for example I've introduced customer newsletters for different businesses so that an email is sent to a customer base, giving them an update on the actions that have been taken as a result of their feedback. Our customers said 'we're having problems with our deliveries', so we worked with our carrier to create a process to improve the standards with their delivery drivers. Our customers said 'your communications don't include all the information I need' so we reviewed and improved all our communications and included the information they need to have about their transaction. These are the type of things that customers really need to hear about, and it will only encourage them to continue using your service and recommend it to others.

Training

Another important aspect of ensuring the voice of the customer is heard is by helping people in your organisation understand what the feedback and metrics collected mean to them and their day to day job. Some people might not know what CSAT or NPS scores are or what is a good score. Some teams or business units might need help facilitating workshops where ideas can be shared and discussed in order to put an action plan in place. The objective is to empower and enable colleagues and provide training and support that is relevant by job level and area of expertise.

Conclusion

A voice of the customer program can help us to truly understand our customers and their experience with our brand. It is great that there are several businesses who have tons of operational data but that is only one side of the story. We also need to be able to understand what our customers like and dislike about our product or service and we need to start offering experiences that are more closely aligned with their needs and expectations. Customers who have a positive experience not only will continue using you, but they will tell others about your product or service which will have an impact on your key performance indicators such as conversion and retention rates.

About Gabriela Geeson MBA, CCXP, CSM
Global Customer Experience and Insights Manager at WorldRemit

Gabriela is Global Customer Experience and Insights Manager at WorldRemit – one of the fastest growing tech companies in Europe. In her role, Gabriela sets the vision for customer experience in over 200 countries across the globe. Gabriela is a talented customer experience professional with over 13 years of experience working across a number of industries - from HealthCare to FinTech. Gabriela focuses on using agile management to deliver experiences that customers want to repeat again and again and share with others. She has led and delivered complex and innovative initiatives to improve Customer Experience and drive Customer Centricity. Gabriela holds an MBA.

Contact

https://www.linkedin.com/in/gabriela-geeson-a5089b2a

Section 6 CX Strategy

Alignment, Communication and Direction

Experiences Don't Matter, Memories Do

Gustavo Imhof

What if we were getting it all wrong?

What if, despite years, nay, decades, of diligent pursuit from some of the brightest customer experience (CX) minds in the world, our understanding of customer experience was still missing a critical component?

With over 8.5 billion dollars spent just on CX software in 2020[1], CX is literally a billion dollars industry. It also is firmly on senior executives' agendas, with several CEO priority reports going as far back as 2013 highlighting CX as one of their key strategic considerations. You would be hard-pressed to find a board which hasn't at least discussed customer experience (although, making it a core priority is another ballgame entirely).

With the two factors above, you would be forgiven to expect the customer experience horror stories were no more and only state of the art experiences would do. Yet, this vision never came to be, and, if we are to believe the anecdotes from the customer experience community since the pandemic began, things have gotten far worse instead.

So, what happened? Why did we not completely transform how businesses interact with their customers? There must be a reason why a field with such significant investments, looked at by brilliant minds and boasting such a high-profile with the top decision-makers has been failing to deliver on its promises after so many years.

I am now convinced we were indeed getting it all wrong. We weren't hitting bullseye for a frighteningly simple and straightforward reason: **we've been aiming at the wrong target!**

If customer experience isn't the right target, what could it possibly be? The answer is: **Memories.**

The Case For A New Focus: Memories Instead Of Experiences

Memory as a topic that has received relatively little attention in CX. Yet, I believe it is nothing less than the missing piece of the puzzle. Ponder the following claim for a second:

The experience your customer has does not have any direct impact on your customers' future behaviours.

The one thing we have all been using to justify investments in customer experience for years has no impact on how your customers will behave, and therefore, your bottom line. In other words, what drives business value through positive word of mouth, repeat business, enhanced loyalty and reduced churn is ***NOT*** customer experience.

No decision has ever been made on the back of a great customer experience. None.

What is it then that drives customer behaviours?

We make decisions and behave based on what we **remember** of said experiences.

If we want to influence our customers' behaviours, we should focus on how people remember experiences, not the experiences themselves.

I know I have made a few several statements that are very controversial and go against the grain of everyone else in CX. Before you discard these as complete nonsenses, let me walk you through a practical example that will make my case more relatable and back these bold statements. This is the story of one of the greatest and most unforgettable dining experiences I have ever had in my life.

Case Study: A London Cabaret

My better half and I wanted to go to a cabaret while we were visiting London and decided to go to *Bunga Bunga*, in Covent Garden. When we walked in, we saw a typically unassuming Italian restaurant, nothing noteworthy. Frankly, I was confused on how this small restaurant could host a cabaret.

We then let the nearby wait staff know we had a booking under the name *Imhof*. They greeted us and took us to our table, or so we thought... We crossed the entire restaurant and faced a discreet black door. A knock on the door and we found ourselves propelled into an epic time travel into the Prohibition Era. Three mobster-looking gentlemen stood on the other side of this door and welcomed us, telling us about *The Don* and how he had a great evening planned for us.

The room they were in very much looked like the freezer at the back of a butcher's shop, with large chunks of meat dangling from the ceiling. They let us through and when the door opened, we were met with a beautiful white marble staircase, the kind you see in movies. At the bottom of the stairs, a Maître D' in tuxedo showed us to our table. We then had a 3-course dinner alongside some genuinely entertaining live acts.

Quite the experience, right? Are you tempted to go there once the pandemic is behind us? I'd recommend it, not for the food, but for the actual experience as a whole.

Now… what if during the live act, they used some magic spell, akin to the neuralyzer in the *Men In Black* movies, that made sure I'd forget the entire night? Putting the ethical and legal dilemmas aside, had I forgotten the evening, would I have been able to share this story with you? No, of course not.

Would I consider going back? Impossible to tell, especially since, in my mind, I would be going there for the first time. After all, I cannot make a decision based on information I do not remember. And neither can your customers because what drives their future behaviours is their memories of experiences. Experiences don't drive decision-making, memories do.

Memories Versus Experiences: Just A Technicality?

Considering everyone in the industry has been obsessing about experiences and perceptions rather than the memories of said experiences, is this technicality even enough for you to consider completely overhauling your CX philosophy?

It all comes down to one fundamental question:

Are memories faithful representations of experiences or in-the-moment perceptions?

To answer this, we turn our attention to an unexpected topic: the legal system. Think about court scenes in literally every movie or legal drama ever, where a direct eyewitness is portrayed as one of the most irrefutable proofs a prosecutor could ever get a hold of. Why? Because we intuitively believe that if someone has experienced something as unusual and as traumatic as witnessing a crime, *they must* be able to remember and vividly recall what they have seen.

It turns out, our intuition is wrong! Thanks to scientific research and the advent of DNA forensics, we now know this kind of testimony is not the smoking gun they were thought out to be.

Here are some crucial facts which science has unveiled:

- 23.7% of lineup identification (several individuals lined up for the eyewitness to identify the culprit) picked the wrong individual in real cases, with real people, about real crimes.[2]
- In laboratory conditions (i.e., simulations without the trauma), 27.9% were misidentified.
- The non-profit The Innocence Project has overturned, thanks to DNA testing, 256 wrongful convictions caused by eyewitness misidentification to date (69% of cases they overturned.[3]
- The majority of the cases above had the actual victim of the crime as the eyewitness.

Let that sink in for a minute. More than 250 people were condemned in the USA for a crime they didn't commit, and that's just those who had their name cleared by The Innocence Project in the last 30 years. At every lineup identification, there is a one in four chance that an innocent person will go through trial and risk prison (or worse). The magnitude and consequences of a fallible memory are spine-chilling.

If things can go this wrong when lives are literally at stake, how can we expect business transactions to somehow be spared this challenge? Customer experiences and the memories of these experiences are not one and the same. If we want to thrive, we need to intentionally design for memorability.

Designing For Memorability: Core Concepts

Designing for memorability is an incredibly vast and complex topic. No one could do it justice in just one chapter. Instead, I'll close this chapter off with an overview of some of the key principles behind what I call *Profitably Memorable Experience Design* as well as some practical ways of implementing these.

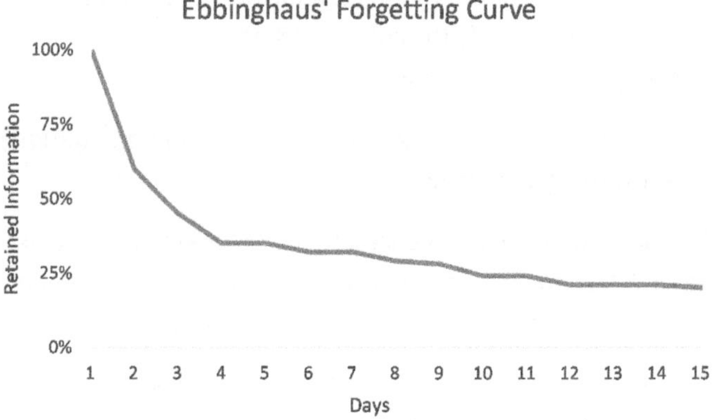

Figure 1 - Concept of the Forgetting Curve based on the work from Hermann Ebbinghaus

Forgetting Curve

The Forgetting Curve[4], is the pillar to memory science. The curve pinpoints that we rapidly forget most of the information we are exposed to and the information we do retain will gradually blur and fade away over time.

The man behind the theory, psychologist Hermann Ebbinghaus discovered there are several factors that make a memory sticky or forgettable, including:

1. The attention and interest given to the experience or information when it first occurred
2. Consolidation of information, i.e., is there repetition to cement the information?
3. Are there cues that can inspire recall?

Want to be remembered? Stand out, grab their attention, create cues, repeat.

Peak-End Rule

Discovered by Nobel Prize winner Daniel Kahneman and colleagues[5], this rule of psychology tells us people don't judge experiences based on a sum or average of all the components of that experience (which is why defining CX as *'the sum of all the experiences'* doesn't help), but rather by focusing on two aspects only: the climax, be it positive or negative, and the conclusion. In other words, the peak and the end of that journey.

To be memorable, we thus need to focus on:

1. The emotional or functional high/low. This can be designed to ensure you create that peak in a positive manner or it could be a pain point in existing journeys (read the next chapter, *The It Depends Trap* from Jessica Noble for more on this).
2. The conclusion of that journey, or did the customer manage to do what they intended to and how did they feel overall at that point in time?

As these two aspects are most likely to be remembered, they are the cornerstone of future customer behaviours – ignore them at your own peril.

Memorable Variables

The brilliant Carmen Simon, PhD lists out 15 levers to make any content memorable and drive action in her book *Impossible To Ignore*[6]. While her research is focused on content specifically, we can borrow some of these levers to design memorable experiences into our to be customer journeys:

1. Context
2. Cues
3. [Contrast]
4. Emotion
5. Facts
6. Familiarity
7. Motivation
8. Novelty
9. Quantity of Info
10. Relevance
11. Repetition
12. [Involvement]
13. Sensory Intensity
14. Social Aspects
15. Surprise

Harnessing these variables, there are several ways you can implement quick wins on your path to becoming more memorable.

- **Repetition.** What's your tagline? If I said *Just do it* you would know who I'm talking about, simply because they remind you at every opportunity.
- **Novelty.** There is a reason innovation is so powerful, it is novel. It also **contrasts** with what is out there already and is often highly **relevant**.
- **Surprise.** Think of proactive (or heroic) service recovery, solving an issue for a customer before they even notice they have a problem. **Emotion** is often involved here.
- **Social Aspects.** Think of the experiments that had people reduce their energy consumption because they were told they consumed more than their neighbours **(Context)**[7].
- **Motivation.** Gamification is about motivating you to achieve an objective. Brands like Fitbit, Duolingo or Plum harness this with brio.
- **Facts.** Use your data to personalise the experience of your customer in ways they may not expect. Great examples include Microsoft's MyAnalytics on wellbeing or Giffgaff telling their customers if they are on the right plan, proactively. Both are monthly examples, breeding repetition that are highly **relevant**.

Together, the forgetting curve, the peak-end rule and the 15 variables give you a powerful starting point as you look at building memorable experiences for your customers, engineering to drive favourable decisions that stick in mind for longer.

As our memorable journey (pun entirely intended) comes to an end, let me ask you one final question:

If you could have the most wonderful, magical and intense evening of your entire life on the condition of having the memory of the evening erased from your mind forever, would you do it? Would it be worth it?

References

1. MarketsAndMarkets, Customer Experience Management Market by Component (Solutions, Services) Touchpoint, Deployment Type, Organization Size, Vertical (IT and Telecom, BFSI, Retail, Healthcare, Media and Entertainment), and Region – Global Forecast to 2025 [website], https://www.marketsandmarkets.com/Market-Reports/customer-experience-management-cem-market-543.html, (accessed 2 February 2021
2. Wells, G. L., Kovera, M. B., Douglass, A. B., Brewer, N., Meissner, C.A. and Wixted, J. T. (2020). Policy and Procedure Recommendations for the Collection and Preservation of Eyewitness Identification Evidence. Law and Human Behaviour, Vol. 44, No 1.
3. The Innocence Project, DNA Exonerations in the United States [website], https://innocenceproject.org/dna-exonerations-in-the-united-states/ {accessed 04 February 2021)
4. Ebbinghaus, H. (1885). Memory: A Contribution to Experimental Psychology. Teachers College, Columbia University
5. Kahneman, D., Fredrickson, B. L., Schreiber, C.A. and Redelmeier, D.A. (1993). When More Pain is Preferred to Less: Adding a Better End. Psychological Science, Vol. 4 No. 6
6. Simon, C. (2016). Impossible to Ignore. McGraw Hill Education.
7. Ayres, I., Raseman, S., Shih, A. (2009) Evidence From Two Large Field Experiments That Peer Comparison Feedback Can Reduce Residential Energy Usage. NBER Working Paper Series, Working Paper 15386

About Gustavo Imhof

Gustavo Imhof was named one of 30 rising stars in customer experience under the age of 30 worldwide thanks to his cross-industry work with customer insight, customer experience strategy and innovation. A prolific speaker, advisor, and writer, he has collaborated with some of the world's biggest brands and has delivered speaking engagements across four continents in French, English and Portuguese.

Gustavo insists on being a full-time practitioner rather than 'just' a consultant. He doesn't believe in designing better experiences for the sake of it, but rather in using customer experience as a lens to improve business performance through unforgettable and profitable experiences.

Indeed, he has been saying for years that customer experience is not just a nice thing to do for customers; it's the best thing to do to propel business performance. This is the cornerstone to his pragmatic and business-led approach in role, through CXAhead as well as the core to his upcoming book due later in 2021.

Contacts And Links

Email: *gustavo@cxahead.com*

Website: *https://www.cxahead.com*

LinkedIn: *https://www.linkedin.com/in/headofcustomerexperience*

The *It Depends* Trap

Jessica Noble, MBA, CCXP

Imagine a room filled with 100+ bank executives gathered for their annual leadership briefing. I had been invited as their keynote speaker to talk about customer experience. Six months earlier, the bank had begun an enterprise-wide transformation, and they were capturing customer feedback after loans and mortgages were funded. As a means of segueing into my keynote, they had handed out six envelopes containing customer quotes to six leaders in the audience. Each person was asked to stand and read their quote aloud. I love customer quotes and am an advocate for sharing them widely.

The first leader stood and read a quote from a mother who had recently closed on the purchase of their first home. She was elated with the outcome and felt their broker helped make their dreams come true!

Customer accolades are gratifying, and the leaders were ready to hear more. The next leader stood and read a quote from a couple who moved cross-country for new jobs. They had to sell a home and buy another simultaneously to fund their new mortgage. Timing had been of the utmost importance. They too were filled with gratitude for each of the bank's team members who helped them through the process and proactively communicated throughout.

They were elated!

The third quote was much the same. I reflected that company meetings like this can be a morale booster, hearing how hard work has paid off.

The next leader stood, but this quote was different. A family had lost out on their dream home and blamed the bank. They felt there was a lack of communication about the process, unwarranted delays, and ultimately funds were not transferred on time. I got a sick feeling in my stomach.

Two more quotes were shared - also indictments of the bank, their cumbersome processes, an absence of timely follow-up, and apparent lack of care for customers.

Their Chief Customer Officer leaned over and confided they had not planned the order of the quotes. The intention was only to share a mix of positive and negative feedback, but the effect of three incredible stories, followed by heartbreak, left a cloud over the room. I was about to be introduced for the keynote. I could rally, but I did not know if the audience could.

A Bank's *It Depends* Experience

How was it possible the bank was so perfectly meeting the needs of some customers and missing the mark so terribly for others?

I did not know specifically at the time why customer experiences were inconsistent, but we would dig deeper later to learn. What I did know was *It Depends* experiences are costly and not uncommon! The experience a customer has should not depend on the day of the week they reach out, the team member(s) they work with, the branch they go to, the channel they choose (self-serve, in person, phone, etc.); you get the picture. Trust is shattered with inconsistency and easily overshadows positive interactions when interactions do not cumulatively achieve a customer's goal.

It Depends experiences are unreliable ones. When a customer's expectation is not met, future experiences are unpredictable and in the absence of certainty, trust is fleeting.

"If you provide a consistent customer experience, customers can rely on that experience. Customers can trust the experience will require the same degree of effort on their part and deliver the same value and the same quality outcome."

- How Customer Experience Analysis Can Uncover Common Blind Spots Killing Profit Margins blog, 2020

Is There A Business Case For Change?

Customer experience is a business strategy, a prime pillar to achieve your corporate vision, versus a corporate action with altruistic motivations. Before we delve into the bank's customer feedback, we must determine where customer experience ranks as a business priority. Successfully making the business case for customer experience and continuing to make it, will determine the long-term success of customer experience as strategy in an organization.

I routinely chat with C-suite thought partners to test the merits of business cases for customer experience. One of my trusted thought partners is Jack Healey, CEO of Bear Hill Advisory Group and former CFO and COO. Jack offered several additional points to make the case for consistency in customer experience.

Let me share highlights from our discussion.

Every company's highest priority is generating revenue and profit - sell more products or services at a better profit margin. There are only two levers to work with: revenue and cost. One of the most significant costs any organization has is attracting new customers. One of the greatest risks to both revenue and cost is retaining existing customers. Keeping those costs and risks in mind is fundamental when building the case.

As Chief Financial Officers (CFOs) are becoming increasingly engaged in strategic decision making and value delivery for organizations, the symptoms related to inconsistent customer experiences do not go unnoticed by most, but the true cost is often masked. If you can expose those costs and lost revenue opportunities, your business case will be made!

Benefits Of Consistency In Customer Experience

Benefits to consider when making the case for consistent customer experiences:

- Existing customers spend more with companies they trust, and reliability and consistency are key aspects of trust.
- Customer complaints decline as satisfaction increases, providing a significant productivity lift for your team.
- The more consistent and positive a customer's experience has been, the more likely they are to overlook a rare experience failure.
- Customers are more likely to make referrals for companies that meet or exceed their expectations regularly.
- Consistent customer experiences reduce the cost of acquiring new customers, thanks to referrals from existing customers.
- Existing customers become less price sensitive, allowing for more flexibility in pricing which can lead to margin improvement.

Jack Healey shared a few other highly correlated (though less direct) considerations based on his experience. These can be valuable discussion points with your executive team:

- Companies with a reputation of customer experience excellence are generally perceived as market leaders, making it easier to execute other business strategies such as acquisitions, debt, and capital formation.

- When bankers and stockholders know of an organization's customer-centric reputation, they are more apt to support its initiatives.
- Loyal customers engage and provide feedback to continuously improve experiences in the most meaningful and valuable ways.
- Customers buy more when their expectations are consistently met, which allows the company to buy inventory from suppliers with volume discounts (better price), leading to more profit.
- Customers who value their relationships are more likely to pay their invoices within business terms.
- Employees are happier and more engaged when their customers are consistently satisfied, and they are not routinely troubleshooting customer escalations.
- A company reputation of happy employees and satisfied customers attracts more qualified talent to expand a growing team.

Opportunity Costs Of *It Depends* Experiences

Opportunity costs (missed opportunities) related to the case for consistency should not be overlooked. Taking opportunity costs into account highlights the risk of choosing to do nothing. When customers have poor experiences, every other key metric in a business will trend in a similar way:

- Costs of sales go up,
- costs of service go up,
- margins go down,
- accounts receivable becomes delinquent,
- inventory turns more slowly, and resources are not fully utilized,
- customer complaints skyrocket and, in turn,

- company morale suffers from handling complaints and processing returns, refunds, and credits, and
- competitors use your *It Depends* experience against you every chance they get!

Diagnosing The Root Of The Problem

Root cause analysis tools are critical as you quickly drill down into the problem and other contributing factors. Many times, we default to informal brainstorming to surface root causes, which oftentimes span silos and functions. Maybe you even cringed a little when I mentioned using a tool. These are not cumbersome tools requiring specialty training, degrees, or certifications but rather simple, lean problem-solving techniques to help dig into the root of complex problems and contributing factors. While there are several you can try, including cause-effect diagram, effect analysis, and failure mode, I often start with the Five Whys method.

To get started, identify symptoms you are seeing or the preliminary problem at hand. Define the problem as clearly as possible, then ask a series of Why questions to drill down into causes and contributing factors. When we stop drilling down after only one or two *Why* questions, we often end up thinking the preliminary root cause is X, when that root cause (X) is actually a symptom (effect) of another problem (Y) versus the primary, core root cause of our initial problem at hand. By asking at least five rounds of *Why* question and using each answer as the basis for the next question, we uncover the linkages between multi-pronged causes.

When we solve for a half-baked root cause, we do not take comprehensive long-term corrective action and do not reap the complete benefits we anticipated when we implemented a solution.

Customer Pain Is A Symptom

As part of the bank's vision to provide industry-leading customer experiences, we conducted a thorough assessment of their employee and customer experiences, processes, technology, and data beginning with their mortgage business. We began by diagnosing problems customers were experiencing and looking for commonalities and trends. The customer quotes read aloud at the leadership event were symptoms; diagnosing the problem and the root cause were crucial.

The problem was the bank was providing an inconsistent experience resulting in too many customers believing they could not count on the bank to meet their expectations. Even among customers who ultimately got their desired outcome (mortgage), many had feedback about specific steps that were frustrating, confusing, or a waste of time.

The quality of this assessment - to diagnose the problem and drill down more deeply into root causes - ultimately determines the success of a proposed solution.

- The banks CFO saw cash flow decreasing at an increasingly concerning rate. Ask why.
- Loan acquisition costs were much higher than their competitors. Ask why.
- Churn in their portfolio was decreasing the overall value to investors. Ask why.
- Keep going. Keep asking why.

Several significant customer pain points and contributing factors were identified including inflating costs to serve customers, lengthening the mortgage process and the customer journey causing customer frustration, and resulting in costly customer churn (purchase abandonment).

Inconsistent experiences were the symptoms of inconsistencies behind the scenes. These were caused by a combination of:

- organizational silos relying on de-centralized data that lacked governance
- self-serve channels relying on disconnected technology
- manual, error-prone processes
- policies and procedures restricting team member empowerment to do the right thing
- undocumented 'workarounds' circumventing time-consuming workflows

Rarely is a single factor the root cause of a complex problem. Single factor causes are often the issues that get fixed while more complex, pervasive problems with many contributing factors are left un-addressed.

Stay Consistent With Your Brand

It is worth noting a consistent customer experience does not mean an assembly line experience. What it does mean is customers experience your company similarly over time.

Think about the chatter that builds up when a new iPhone launches. A couple of years ago, there was a lot of feedback that the new iPhone was not much better, and Androids were closing the gap. This type of chatter happened because customers expect innovation from Apple. Whether customers expect innovation, disruption, luxurious levels of personalization, or a do-it-yourself experience, you must provide that type of experience reliably and consistently.

Listen For The *It Depends*

Would you go to ________ store or ________ restaurant again? Would you buy ________ SaaS (software), if you were making the decision all over again? Would you work with ________ vendor next time? Would you recommend ________ product to a friend?

Listen to your front-line team members. Listen to your customers. Listen for the *It Depends* as you hear customer complaints and read their feedback. Prioritize investing the time and energy to get it right and to keep getting it right consistently to build lifetime customers.

"Value preservation and value creation are the responsibility of management. By eliminating the It Depends in customer delivery - revenues grow, rather than erode; customer acquisition costs decline, rather than grow; return on invested capital grows as less is required for value preservation and more can be invested in value creation."

– Jack Healey, CEO Bear Hill Advisory

Avoid the *It Depends* trap by designing and delivering experiences customers can rely on. Be the company customers can trust because they know their experience will be consistent, whether online or in person, regardless of the time of year, or the department they are interacting with.

Citation

- Noble. J. (2020). *How Customer Experience Analysis Can Uncover Common Blind Spots Killing Profit Margins.* Magnetic Experiences. www.magneticexperiences.com/blog/customer-experience-analysis

About Jessica Noble, MBA, CCXP

Jessica Noble is an industry-recognized Customer Experience and Business Strategy Executive as well as a Fractional Chief Customer Officer (CCO) who is passionate about helping small and mid-size businesses develop strong, sustainable profit margins with actionable strategies as they scale by plugging money leaks and elevating both employee and customer experiences.

She is the founder of Magnetic Experiences an international business strategy and customer experience coaching and consulting firm, currently serving clients in the North American, Africa and Asia. Jessica is also the author of The Five Customer Experience Mistakes Causing Profit Erosion.

Jessica was driving business strategy and customer experience optimization and transformation throughout organizations for nearly two decades before launching Magnetic Experiences. She has 15 years' experience providing consulting and business advisory services for midsize to Fortune 50 companies and began her customer experience career leading an agent experience redesign for Nationwide.

Contacts And Links

Email: *info@magneticexperiences.com*

Website: *www.magneticexperiences.com*

Facebook: *https://www.facebook.com/MagneticExperiences*

Instagram: *https://www.instagram.com/magneticexperiences/*

LinkedIn: *https://www.linkedin.com/in/jessicajnoble/*

Twitter: *https://twitter.com/MagneticExp*

Service Excellence: Create A Customer Focused Value Generating Engine Of Your Business

Gregorio Uglioni – the CX Goalkeeper

Introduction

Alice is asking herself where her new jogging shoes are as she bought them online ten days ago and the online shop promise was: we deliver within one week.

Her husband, Bob, needs a new PIN code for his credit card as he entered the wrong one already three times in a row.

Charles, a good friend of Bob, receives a push message in his mobile banking app asking him to confirm his residential address.

Finally, Debra, Charles' partner, is looking to cancel her subscription to a business newspaper as she has realized that she has no time to read it.

These four protagonists, representing generic customers, are facing different situations with a common denominator: they are all about to experience how companies serve their customers. All of them are hoping to have their needs met in a fast, easy and convenient way (Dodkins, 2020). They would love to be treated as human beings and not merely as a case or like a number.

It is important to note that 42% of customers decreased or completely stopped spending with a company after experiencing a single poor interaction (Dorsey & Segall, 2020) whilst 62% of the customers are willing to pay more for good customer service (Hyken, 2020).

Customer service is one of the three key components (alongside brand promise and value proposition) which drive customer loyalty. A consistent and superior level of customer service is the key differentiator in today's world if a company wants to stand out against competitors selling more and more comparable products. To be clear, we are not speaking about just creating happy customers but instead about deploying a customer centric strategy to improve acquisition, enhance retention and drive share of wallet whilst decreasing costs. (Dodkins, 2020).

The Challenge

How should companies structure their service offering? How is it possible to balance customers' and shareholders' expectations? Companies always strive to optimize their profits. Tragically, the easiest and fastest way to reduce cost is to reduce the number of employees in the customer service centre. The service department is often considered as an old-fashioned and significant cost centre, with lots of people and therefore a high proportion of labour cost. Unfortunately, the consequences of such cost-cutting initiatives are known. They can frequently create a vicious circle from which it is difficult to break free. Consequences include a decreasing number of serviced customers, corresponding in worsening service quality, an increasing number of contacts (e.g., re-callers) and employee stress leading to unhappy employees and customers with high risk of attrition for both.

The Proposed Solution

In the following section, I propose a holistic model to transform service departments from a cost centre into a value generating customer focused engine for the business. The focus is on how to strategically define, execute and optimize service interactions to create WIN-WIN-WIN situations by creating value for the company, customers and employees, all at the same time.

A Model To Optimize Customer Interactions

The model describes how to strategically achieve service excellence by leveraging the following three enablers while applying the Value Irritant Matrix (VIM) to customer interactions. When the VIM was developed in 2008 (Price & Jaffe, 2008) these enablers were not as advanced as they are today, and enhancements since then make the VIM tool even more powerful.

The Three Enablers

- **Exploit available data** to obtain insights about customers (always remaining compliant to existing rules and regulations, e.g., GDPR in Europe). Companies hold a lot of unused data which can be utilized for several purposes, e.g., to better understand customers and to learn from their behaviour, in order to create better and more personalized customer experiences whilst also supporting the employees servicing them.
- **Leveraging technology** as a means to offer superior service. Today, several solutions (e.g., Artificial Intelligence, omnichannel orchestration tool, CRM) are mature enough to be either directly available to customers (e.g., chatbot and voicebot) or to be fully exploited within service departments (e.g., CRM, Robotic Process Automation). These technologies can potentially create significantly better customer experiences compared to 20 years ago.

- **Betting on game-changing human to human interactions.** Customer facing employees remain a key success factor for companies. Therefore, they should be empowered to empathize with customers, to independently decide on appropriate actions to be taken to solve customer issues and to create added value for the customer and the company.

The Value Irritant Matrix

The VIM was created by Bill Price, first Vice President of Customer Service at Amazon. It analyses the value of an interaction from both the company and the customer points of view (Price, 2018).

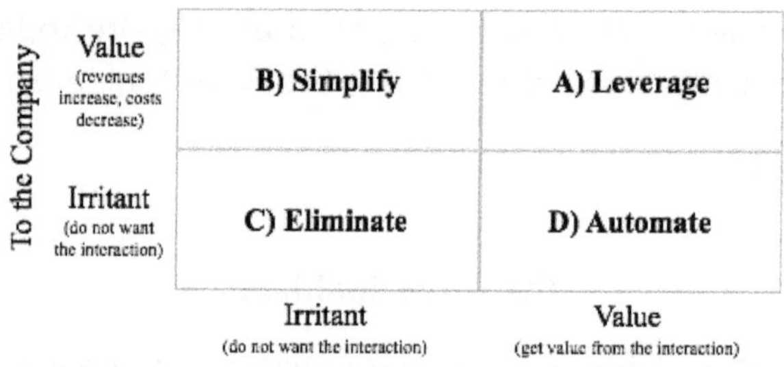

Figure 1. The Value Irritant Matrix, own representation based on (Price, 2018).

By leveraging the customer's journey, it is possible to identify all existing interaction opportunities and classify them using this matrix. By doing this, it is possible to understand if a dialogue either creates a value or is irritating to either side. Based on this dialogue classification, the organisation can define different strategies on how to handle all interactions independently from the channel. The resulting four different options are depicted in the four quadrants of the matrix above.

These then translate into the four strategies as follows:

Note: The VIM classification is industry dependent. For example, an address change for a bank can be "irritating", whereas for an insurance this could generate new business opportunities (e.g., offering new products).

A) Leverage (company: value, customer: value)

The first quadrant relates to Debra's example. She wants to cancel her subscription. This case generates a value to her and a cross-selling opportunity for the company, even if they have divergent objectives (for Debra in ending an unnecessary subscription, for the organisation in retaining Debra as a customer). Keeping an existing customer is often cheaper than finding new ones.

How can companies leverage such interactions?

- Structure dialogues in a smart way by finding overlap between their respective objectives, making them both happy.
- Transform interactions into value generating opportunities which can reduce churn rates as well as lead to upselling/cross selling. Satisfied customers often spread good word of mouth which in turn can drive lower costs of new customer acquisition.
- Empower employees to be the real differentiator and brand ambassadors.

Data and technology should support employees during customers interactions (e.g., predicting the next best action or how to avoid the next disruption or the most appropriate offering).

A suggested solution for our example: Employees could offer the podcast or a digital version of the newspaper to fulfil Debra's need to get a business update during her sport sessions.

A smart real-life solution: Zappos contact centre (call them and you will find out the real value of a human-to-human interaction).

B) Simplify (company: value, customer: irritating)

Let us think about Charles' case. He was asked by his bank to confirm his address: such an interaction is irritating for him ("why should I confirm my address?") and creates value mainly for the bank (which requires the address for compliance reasons).

How can companies simplify such interactions?

- Make them easy, fast and convenient for the customers.
- Use the customers' preferred channel.

This can be achieved by using available data (e.g., identifying customer preferences) and technology solutions. Humans should not be involved in such interactions.

A suggested solution for our example: Charles could receive a push message in the banking app, with a very short note explaining the reason for this interaction. The app represents a secure channel which has already been used several times: with one click, Charles could confirm his prefilled address and the case could be completed to the satisfaction of both parties involved.

A smart real-life solution: Apple's FaceID to authorise the download of apps.

C) Eliminate (company: irritating, customer: irritating)

Let us come back to Alice's missing shoes. She is really upset having not received her order. Also, this is irritation for the organisation. Nobody achieves any value.

How can companies eliminate such interactions?

- Proactively inform the customer throughout the process, quickly identify and definitively fix root causes.

Expectations setting and process stability are key success factors to offer a consistent experience. Data should be leveraged to discover such broken process. Employees should not have to be involved in such interactions as much as possible.

A suggested solution for our example: the online shop should stick to the delivery promise and deliver on time. Clearly communicate the progress of the delivery status, and proactively inform Alice about any unexpected delays.

A smart real-life solution: Amazon Prime's delivery promise (e.g., within one day for selected products).

D) Automate: (company: irritating, customer: value)

This is the case of Bob: he needs a new PIN for his credit card. For him this is valuable. However, for the company this process has no value added (as they need to identify the customer, generate the new pin and send it to him in a secure way.)

How can companies automate such interactions?

- Offer an automated process that customers can use 24/7 no matter where they are.

Data and technology are the key elements to properly offering self-service to customers. Humans can add minimum value to such interactions.

A suggested solution for our example: Bob could request the new PIN for the card through WhattsApp or another secure channel for which he has already been authenticated.

A smart real-life solution: Revolut showing the PIN code of the card in the app.

One Last Improvement: "Prevention Is Better Than Cure" Applied to Customer Service

An interaction can be initiated in one of two ways: by the company (proactively) or by the customer (reactive, the usual way of doing business).

It is important to understand that by leveraging data and technology, companies can proactively engage with customers, and surprise them in a positive way. Closer relationships improve customer engagement and their financial value. It is proven that engaged customers spend more.

In our example, why did the online shop not inform Alice about the delivery delay? And why did the bank not inform Bob that his card had been blocked as a preventive measure?

There are many other valuable examples of "proactive maintenance" and communication in the market showing the power of predictive engagement, e.g., machines with Internet Of Things sensors which automatically inform in real-time if something is not working properly without waiting for a human to identify the issue.

Key-Learnings

To summarize these discussion points:

1. Reducing staffing levels and "squeezing the lemon" is a short-term measure to reduce cost, which can lead to a deterioration in customer relationships and therefore financial impact in the long term (e.g., customer churn).

2. Data, technology and the human touch are key enablers to improve the service experience. Through rapid development in the areas of data and technology these enablers have become more and more accessible to business of all sizes.

3. Being proactive remains a game-changer to this day but customers are becoming more accustomed to and expect great, carefully thought-through proactive experiences.

4. The VIM helps to set the focus on value interactions from both points of view: the customer and the company - this can be a gamechanger in how you look at your customer journeys.

5. High quality service can be a key differentiator and when applied in a strategic manner creates value and reduces costs.

...and remember: there is no second chance to make a good first impression!

Bibliography

- Hyken, S., 2020. The 2020 ACA Survey: Achieving Customer Amazement: Shep Hyken.

- Price, B. & Jaffe, D., 2008. The Best Service is No Service: Jossey-Bass.

- Price, B., 2018. Customer Think. [Online] Available at: https://customerthink.com/the-best-service-is-no-service-turns-10-going-strong/ [Accessed 3 January 2020].

- Dorsey, M. & Segall, D., 2020. What Happens After a Bad Experience, 2020: XM Institute, Qualtrics.

- Dodkins, J., 2020. ACXS Certification. [Online] Available at: https://www.acxs-online.com [Accessed 4 February 2020].

About Gregorio Uglioni

Gregorio is an expert in Business Transformation, Innovation and Customer Experience. Thanks to his strong leadership skills, Gregorio has successfully led several transformation programs achieving great results, creating a positive customer impact while relentlessly nurturing a positive innovation culture. His cross-industry engagement for the development of the customer experience science (e.g., with his podcast "CX Goalkeeper") and his in-depth know-how allowed him to be recognized as an expert in Customer Experience.

He is one of the few CCXP's in Switzerland and the world's first certified ACXSPlus. Gregorio holds two masters' degrees from the University of Zurich. He started his career at Accenture and is now the Head of Business Excellence and Customer Experience at Swisscard AECS GmbH.

Gregorio's battery charger is his family.

In this chapter Gregorio is expressing his own views.

Contacts And Links

www.cxgoalkeeper.com

https://www.linkedin.com/in/gregorio-uglioni/

The Podcast «CX Goalkeeper» is available on all major podcast platforms (Apple, Google, Amazon and Spotify)

Why Diversify Your CX Strategy?

Mandisa Makubalo

Introduction

For years it seems very easy to generalize and think of customers as one country. It also seems like human nature for businesses to group, stereotype and categorize in an attempt to understand and simply easier not to unpack the nuances of the township economy. Oversimplifying and generalizing in an attempt to understand the complexity of the township economy business landscape is where businesses lose ground. The township economy is very different with different behaviors to overall South African customer behaviors and businesses need to diversify their CX strategy.

Case Study

Siphenathi is a 35 year old black woman living in the township of Gugulethu in Cape Town, South Africa. She has a degree in Masters of Business Administration and currently works as a Head of Department in one of South Africa's largest petro-chemical companies where she earns a salary of between R900k – R1.5 million per annum. She is a single mother with two beautiful children, living with her mom and two siblings in her house which is financed through a mortgage bond of 20 years and she drives a financed motor vehicle. Siphenathi falls in the black middle class group namely the black diamond market segment which consists of approximately three million black middle-class South Africans with a buying power of approximately R200 billion (Anon., 2008).

She is a premium customer in one of South Africa's top five financial institutions which means she has access to a range of banking options including lending, savings, investments, financial planning along with exclusive rewards and lifestyle offers. The qualifying criteria for a premier account is an annual salary of between R350 000 – R949 999.

Siphenathi hardly visits the bank, she performs most of her banking online and telephonically through the help of her private banker. On the odd occasion when she really has to physically visit the bank, she has to drive to the city because of lack of private banking solutions in the township. After 12 years of banking with this financial institution the bank made a decision to integrate its products and services to the township of Gugulethu in one of the local shopping centres. The banking hall was set up with the normal banking solutions including a relationship banking section which is designed for premium customers. Siphenathi is excited about this integration because it's convenient for her, she literally can now walk to the bank as the shopping centre is situated five minutes away from home. She reaches out to her private banker and is surprised to learn that he is not aware of the relationship banking solution offered in this branch and finds this quite odd.

Whilst visiting the bank she learns that there is no relationship banker readily available, she is asked to wait for the bank manager who is also not available. She finds that every time she visits the bank the relationship banking section is closed resulting in her being redirected to the long queues of savings, silver and gold account holders.

A few months after opening its doors the branch closed down

to the public to undergo renovations without any notification to its customers. After a period of two months the bank re-opens, this time the size of the bank is half its original size. The downsizing included a complete removal of the relationship banking solution, three service consultants, three bank tellers and five automated machines (with three of the machines allowing for cash deposits and the rest of the machines do not allow for deposits, they only allow withdrawals and bank statement retrievals).

Siphenathi represents a customer segment that is based in one of the many townships of South Africa, these customer segments are always served as a country forced to accept what brands have to offer. Most brands integrate products and services to the township economy promising customers a positive experience and yet these customers are only able to access these experiences by traveling to the city.

The Problem

Many businesses like the financial institution mentioned in the above case study often stereotype customers, even when it is their own customer for their own industry.

I have personally experienced businesses especially the financial services industry taking a holistic perspective and approach to serving township customers. These brands would apply over simplified segmentation models rather than seek true understanding of the customers with whom they are engaging.

Looking at customers through the lens of behaviors alone is not enough, township customers like any other customers have needs and wants that require a diversified strategy.

Photo - Mandisa Makubalo Gugulethu, Cape Town, South Africa. 2021

Photo - Mandisa Makubalo, Gugulethu, Cape Town, South Africa 2021

The conventional approach to CX strategy fails for these five reasons:

- **Thinking for the customer** – with CX strategy being an "actionable plan in place to deliver delightful and meaningful experiences across every interaction a customer has with your business", most brands think for customers rather than allowing customers to think for themselves. There is a difference in how brands think customers want to feel and how customers actually want to feel.
- **Fails to represent the customer diversity** – a handful of people planning and strategizing in a virtual meeting for a week will not be able to understand all the factors influencing customer behaviors.
- **Leaves out the voice of the customer** – the customer's voice is missing and at times if represented, the representation is minimal. The focus is always on the market, competition, industry, financial performance and less on the customers.
- **Leadership Biases** – there are leadership biases that prevent critical stakeholders from being part of the solution, these stakeholders are perceived as part of the problem.
- **Rigorous and Stringent** – the uncompromising inflexibility of business leaders in a fast-changing world is doing great harm to customers resulting in great risks for businesses as most of the strategies prove hard to implement.

The Recommended Solution

The global pandemic has caused a spike in the number of unprecedented challenges for businesses, forcing them to consider customer needs and behaviors at every stage of decision making. The proposed solution is a framework to do just that, in a structured approach. It involves empathy, defining, ideation, prototyping and testing to strategy design. Stages like "empathize" make this methodology unique in designing diversified customer experience strategies, but it is the focus on humans and their behavior that makes it most effective. The proposed solution is applying the Design Thinking methodology to designing a diversified customer experience strategy.

DESIGN THINKING FOR DIVERSE CX STRATEGY

MANDISA MAKUBALO

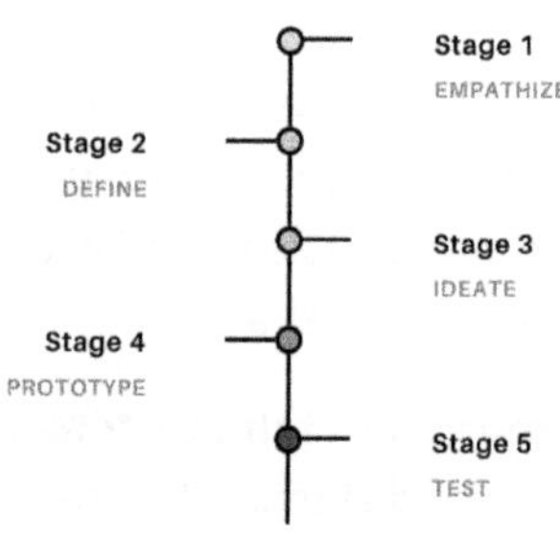

Design Thinking doesn't depend much on historical data but encourages futuristic resolutions for customers. It is time for businesses to rethink their CX strategies by taking a human centric approach to the design process. Considering that these stages require a good amount of focus on the customers, this methodology proves to be immensely helpful in getting businesses to not only develop deep empathy for their customers but to also create strategies that meet a specific need. With the South African population being made up of diverse origins, cultures and a total of 11 official spoken languages customer experience strategies must reflect in-depth understanding and care for these nuances in order to be effective.

According to Stats SA, 80% of South Africa's population is black South Africans, whose collective buying power is R335 billion. There is a black middle class also known as the black diamonds that emerged in 2005 with a collective buying power of R180 billion and 77% of them still live in South African townships. Brands that seek to understand the requirements and needs of such diverse customer markets become effective in designing diverse CX strategies.

By nature a strategy is a plan of action designed to achieve a long term goal, it creates vision and direction for the whole organization, it is important that all people within the company are following the same direction. The very same goes for a CX strategy because this is the action plan in place to deliver positive and meaningful experiences across the interactions a customer has with a brand.

Let us look at the attributes of each of the design thinking stages as it relates to creating a diverse CX strategy:

Empathize

- Here the brand seeks to understand the customer in terms of who they are and what matters to them as a customer. Through this stage brands uncover emotions, seek stories and most importantly this is done in a non-judgemental manner. Brands conduct interviews and shadow their customers with the overall objective of truly seeking to understand them. It is out of this process that brands can truly unfold the diversity in their customers and begin to use the outcomes of this process to truly know the positive and meaningful experiences their customers are seeking across every interaction.

Define

- This stage of the process allows brands to create a point of view based on the above customer insights and needs which will result in a human centric problem statement. A diverse CX strategy is one that is able to identify with the tensions, pain points and challenges customers encounter across the different interaction points. This is where the required diversity is achieved.

Ideate

- Through this stage brands are able to share ideas, suspend all judgements concerning what customers want and need. At this stage all ideas are seen as worthy and begin to be prioritized before the creation of a mock-up CX strategy.

Prototype

- In this stage brands start creating simple mock-ups and storyboards of the CX strategy before its implementation. It is important that brands are able to create experiences and role play to understand context prior to communicating it with the business and customers.

Testing

- The testing stage involves the process of testing with customers to gather additional data, gain deeper empathy, embrace failure, understand impediments, test what works and what doesn't work with the strategy and iterate quickly.

Conclusion

A customer experience strategy is often confused with a business strategy, in most cases brands define the CX strategy for the customer rather than allowing customers to define their strategy through the above methodology. Design thinking is anchored in understanding customer's needs and pulling together what is desirable from a human point. It challenges assumptions, redefines problems and encourages brands to focus on the people they are creating for, it is for this reason I recommend adapting this methodology as a key to creating a diverse CX strategy.

... remember, customers are diverse by nature and a meaningful CX strategy is one that embraces this diversity!

Bibliography

- http://www.statssa.gov.za/ [Accessed 09 February 2021]
- https://www.statista.com [Accessed 05 February 2021]
- https://careerfoundry.com/en/blog/ux-design/what-is-design-thinking-everything-you-need-to-know-to-get-started/ [Accessed 06 February 2021]

About Mandisa Makubalo

Mandisa Makubalo is an experienced business leader and management consultant in the disciplines of customer experience management, strategic thinking, business continuity planning and change management. Her previous corporate and client-focused experience has elevated the business results and operations of leading companies in multiple industries across South Africa. She is the Founder of South Africa's first 100% black owned CX management consultancy, Unlimited Experiences SA (*www.theunlimitedco.com*), situated in the township of Philippi in the beautiful City of Cape Town known for the iconic Table Mountain. Mandisa Makubalo has been instrumental in the development of the township economy in South Africa by working with local businesses in driving sustainable growth through customer experience management. Her recent success includes being appointed as Expert Advisor for the Akro Capital Township Accelerate Programme working with over 50 township entrepreneurs across South Africa and her recent appointment as Founding Member of the Women in CX global community.

In this chapter Mandisa is expressing her own professional views.

Contacts And Links

LinkedIn: *https://www.linkedin.com/in/mandisa-makubalo-9b180b6b*

Email: *mandisa@theunlimitedco.com*

Three Keys To Customer Experience For Platform Businesses

Anna Noakes Schulze

We're living in a time of tremendous disruption. Even before the global pandemic, the business world faced at least two major sources of business disruption: digital transformation and the platform revolution. The customer experience (CX) profession has been deeply engaged in digital transformation while largely ignoring the rise of platform businesses. Now it's time for CXers to see the bigger picture. I'll tell you how platform business models took over the world in less than a generation, what makes them so different, and why digital transformation alone won't ensure business survival. I'll describe why CX is rooted in pipeline business models and how it needs to adapt to the new and emerging business models of the digital economy. Finally, I'll show you how to leverage the three keys to CX success for platform businesses.

The entire knowledge base of CX was designed around classic pipeline businesses that create goods and services along a one-way linear value chain from suppliers to producers to consumers/ customers. Retailers, hotels, and linear television are all typical examples. For most pipeline businesses, operational efficiency and optimizing business activities centered on attracting, serving and retaining customers are the levers of success.

In the 21st century, the greatest source of business innovation and growth is coming from platform businesses. Amazon, Airbnb and YouTube are all examples of platforms. A platform is "a business based on enabling value-creating interactions between external producers and consumers"[1] in a technology-enabled digital ecosystem. Instead of owning the products and services they offer, platforms act as connectors between two or more groups of users, such as hosts and guests on Airbnb.[2] It's important to note that platforms are not just a technology, or a software suite or any kind of online business.[3] Platforms are a fundamentally different category of business model.

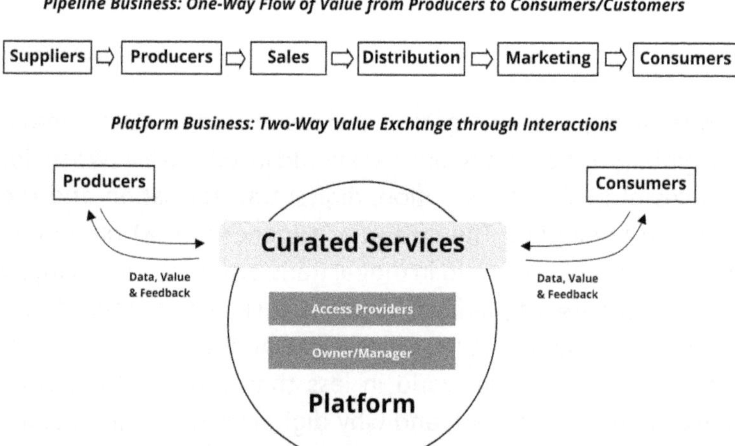

Figure 1: Pipelines vs Platforms[4] © 2021 Anna Noakes Schulze

Many of the greatest startup success stories of the past two decades have been platforms, including household names like Uber and TripAdvisor. Just ten years ago pipeline businesses dominated the top ten biggest companies in the world by market capitalization. Today, platforms are eight of the top ten.[5] So how did such a massive shift happen so quickly? The simple reason is this: platforms beat pipelines every time.[6]

From an investor perspective, platforms have some significant advantages over traditional pipeline businesses in terms of scalable growth, lower cost structures, higher returns and greater profitability. Investors consistently value platforms at higher multiples as well: nearly 9x revenues for platforms versus 2-4x revenues for pipelines.[7] Worldwide, platforms are nearly 60% of all unicorns,[8] meaning privately held startups valued at $1 billion or more. That's not just a trend. The Word Economic Forum estimates that 70% of new value created in the economy over the next decade will be based on digitally enabled platform business models.[9]

Now let's start to break down some of the key differences between pipelines and platforms. Pipelines are businesses that create value internally by converting inputs from suppliers into products and services which employees deliver to customers in a well-defined linear value chain. Pipeline businesses depend on generating sales, operating efficiency and a conversion funnel that turns prospects into customers and retains as many as possible for repeat business and advocacy.

But now pipelines are losing ground to platforms. Platform businesses create or unlock value externally by delivering products and services via networks of collaboration and exchange.[10] Instead of four walls and a linear value chain they involve entire digital ecosystems that support two-way interactions between producers and consumers/customers. A marketplace platform like Amazon can include not only their own products but those of many other partners or even direct competitors.

In Platform Revolution, authors Parker, Van Alstyne and Choudary describe the three fundamental shifts going from pipelines to platforms:[11]

1. **From resource control to resource orchestration**
   E.g., hotels own the buildings and rooms that they control, but Airbnb organizes access to buildings and rooms owned by others.

2. **From internal optimization to external interaction**
   E.g., traditional retailers use customer journey mapping to optimize customer engagement, but platforms use governance (meaning a set of rules, practices and design elements) to optimize user engagement.

3. **From focus on customer value to focus on ecosystem value**
   E.g., pipelines are concerned with maximizing the total revenue from each customer as customer lifetime value (CLV) but platforms strive to maximize the total ecosystem value, meaning value co-created through the interactions of all platform participants.

Platforms tend to beat pipelines due to a crucial difference in how they grow and scale.[12] In pipeline businesses, the people and resources needed to increase revenues generally increase the operating costs as well, so the business will tend toward linear, monotone growth. By contrast, platform businesses are products of the information age. They tend to be digital-first businesses that are data rich and asset light.[13] But their major advantage is the way they leverage positive feedback loops called network effects[14] for exponential growth. Simply put, network effects refer to "the impact that the number of users has on the value created for each user."[15] Generally, the more participants on both sides of a platform, the more valuable the platform becomes for everyone.

The Amazon Flywheel is a famous example of a platform growth engine powered by network effects.[16] It's a virtuous circle of more leading to more: more sellers and more offerings enhance the customer experience. More customers generate traffic that attracts more sellers with more offerings. The selling side benefits from market access and high traffic while the customer side benefits from better selection and lower prices. Unlike pipelines, platform businesses are able grow and scale exponentially because each new user increases the overall value of the platform while adding negligible marginal cost.[17]

Figure 2: Amazon Flywheel Benefits CX and PX © 2021 Anna Noakes Schulze

Not every platform business was born that way. Companies can evolve from pipelines to platforms or become a hybrid of both. Even John Deere, the world's number one manufacturer of farming equipment, has found a second life in a bold transition from venerable product-centered business to cutting-edge platform business. The company's MyJohnDeere platform uses software products to connect their equipment and other machines with owners, operators, dealers, and agricultural consultants. Sensor data combined with historical data is shared with stakeholders over the platform to help farmers manage their fleet, improve efficiency, and reduce costs. It's a great example of how platform businesses use rich data streams to create more value for their customers and identify new sources of revenue.[18]

For customer experience professionals, it's worth taking a moment to appreciate just how powerful this is as a loyalty driver. Normally it would be an easy decision to switch brands and buy a different tractor. But what if your tractor is networked to all of your other equipment and you have access to real-time data essential to running a successful farm? Now the cost of switching is very high. The brilliance of John Deere's platform strategy is how it leverages ecosystem partners to create new value for customers and partners, discourage brand switching, and promote long-term loyalty.

Here I'd like to offer you a practical approach to platform businesses from a customer experience perspective. CX is generally not the primary focus of the platform community, but there are some valuable clues that can signpost our way. I've distilled these into a simple framework that will help customer experience professionals leverage customer and partner experience as a business driver in platform environments.

My approach involves three essential keys to platform experience: Value, Usability and Trust.

- **Value** means that the platform offers a core interaction that solves a real problem for both sides, such as Uber's core interaction: allowing drivers offering rides and passengers seeking rides to interact with each other. Value also means that there are mechanisms to capture, monetize and reward value creation on the platform; and that the platform is able to respond dynamically to evolve the offerings to better serve user needs.

- **Usability** means that platform users enjoy an excellent user experience[19] emphasizing well-known heuristics like convenience, ease of use, consistency, learnability, system speed and reliability, clear and simple error prevention and/or recovery, help, and user guides. In addition, usability would have to include platform-appropriate filtering, matching and communications functionality.

- **Trust** means designing pillars of digital trust so that platform participants can confidently interact with each other and exchange value.[20] Platforms can't function without some level of trust between various participants and also between the participants and the platform itself.[21] Important trust considerations must include data security and privacy, user identification, secure payment systems, and appropriate standards for user-generated content such as listings, ratings, and reviews.

Each of these three keys (Value, Usability and Trust) has an important role to play in supporting active participation and overall platform health:

1. First, by attracting and engaging users with a core interaction that speaks to their needs,
2. Second, by offering interactions and value exchange with minimal friction to keep users active on the platform,
3. Third, by reducing the perception of risk and enabling trusted transactions, and
4. Fourth, by generating the kind of positive emotional experiences that are proven to drive loyalty and retention in platform environments.[22]

So where does this leave us? Pipeline businesses won't be going away any time soon, but they'll be increasingly vulnerable to disruption by platform businesses. Platforms have unique advantages that allow them scale up quickly, create new markets, disrupt old ones, and find novel solutions to adding or unlocking value. When a pipeline meets a platform, the platform business almost always wins.

Despite the pandemic, the world is not going to stand still. Businesses that want to survive and thrive will have to start investing where it matters. They will need to push ahead with digital transformation and modernize legacy systems that keep customer data siloed. They will also need to identify opportunities to adopt a digital ecosystem mindset and either build, buy or join scalable digital platforms. This is going to involve a fundamental business shift from producing value to orchestrating value co-creation in digital ecosystems.

"In the twenty-first century, the supply chain is no longer the central aggregator of business value. What a company owns matters less than what it can connect".
- Applico

Digital transformation is an important first step for legacy businesses that want to remain competitive in the digital economy but it's just the beginning. According to research from McKinsey, more than 30% of global economic activity could be mediated by platforms in the next five years. But only 3% of established companies have an effective platform strategy.[23] This is a huge vulnerability that business leaders will have to address.

If CX is to continue being an effective business driver in platform environments we will need to understand that platform experience isn't just about the customer experience (the demand side); it's also about the partner experience (the supply side). Building a platform business means understanding the needs of both sides of the market and bringing them together effectively to encourage interactions and value exchange.

We'll need to adapt our core competencies, methods and tools to suit the unique characteristics, drivers and KPIs of platform business models. This includes less reliance on some of our familiar, standardized metrics of pipeline businesses and more on platform-specific metrics.[24] We'll need to get out of our comfort zone, learn from related disciplines and innovate how we practice CX now and into the future. In a digital, data-driven, networked economy, you can't succeed without understanding what platforms do and how they work.[25]

Make no mistake: going from pipelines to platforms means having less direct control over the customer experience (and partner experience) than we've been accustomed to. Everything changes once you start pulling value into an ecosystem instead of pushing it out through a linear value chain. When the business models change or evolve then the way we do CX needs to evolve as well. My three keys to platform experience can offer a useful starting point for understanding how to leverage the overall customer and partner experience as a platform business driver. These three keys to attracting, serving and retaining active platform users are Value, Usability and Trust.

References

1. Parker, Geoffrey G., Van Alstyne, Marshall W., and Choudary, Sangeet Paul, *Platform Revolution: How Networked Markets Are Transforming the Economy--and How to Make Them Work for You*, New York, W.W. Norton & Company, 2016.
2. van Dijck, José , Poell, Thomas, and de Waal, Martijn, *Platform Society: Public Values in a Connective World*, Oxford University Press, 2018.
3. Moazed, Alex, and Johnson, Nicholas L., *Modern Monopolies: What it Takes to Dominate the 21st Century Economy*, New York, St. Martin's Press, 2016.
4. Thank you to Marshall W. Van Alstyne and Hamidreza Hosseini for their input on this graphic.
5. The Visual Capitalist, "The 10 Most Valuable Brands in the World," inforgraphic posted at https://www.visualcapitalist.com/ranked-the-most-valuable-brands-in-the-world/
6. Parker, Geoffrey G., Van Alstyne, Marshall W., and Choudary, Sangeet Paul, *Platform Revolution: How Networked Markets Are Transforming the Economy--and How to Make Them Work for You*, New York, W.W. Norton & Company, 2016.
7. Moazed, Alex, and Johnson, Nicholas L., *Modern Monopolies: What it Takes to Dominate the 21st Century Economy*, New York, St. Martin's Press, 2016.

8. Cusumano, Michael A., Yoffie, David B., and Gawer, Annabelle, "The Future of Platforms," MIT Sloan Management Review, Spring 2020.

9. Mast, Steve, "Are Digital Ecosystems The Secret To Building And Growing A Strong Economy?" Forbes Technology Council post, August, 20, 2020 at: https://www.forbes.com/sites/forbestechcouncil/2020/08/20/are-digital-ecosystems-the-secret-to-building-and-growing-a-strong-economy/

10. Parker, Geoffrey G., Van Alstyne, Marshall W., and Choudary, Sangeet Paul, *Platform Revolution: How Networked Markets Are Transforming the Economy--and How to Make Them Work for You*, New York, W.W. Norton & Company, 2016.

11. Van Alstyne, Marshall W., Parker, Geoffrey G., and Choudary, Sangeet Paul, "Pipelines, Platforms, and the New Rules of Strategy," Harvard Business Review, April 2016.

12. Parker, Geoffrey G., Van Alstyne, Marshall W., and Choudary, Sangeet Paul, *Platform Revolution: How Networked Markets Are Transforming the Economy--and How to Make Them Work for You,* New York, W.W. Norton & Company, 2016.

13. Cusumano, Michael A., Gawer, Annabelle, and Yoffie, David B., *The Business of Platforms: Strategy in the Age of Digital Competition, Innovation, and Power*, New York, Harper Business, 2019.

14. *Ibid.*

15. Parker, Geoffrey G., Van Alstyne, Marshall W., and Choudary, Sangeet Paul, *Platform Revolution: How Networked Markets Are Transforming the Economy--and How to Make Them Work for You*, New York, W.W. Norton & Company, 2016.

16. For an overview of the Amazon Flywheel see: https://www.ecomcrew.com/amazon-flywheel/

17. Moazed, Alex, and Johnson, Nicholas L., *Modern Monopolies: What it Takes to Dominate the 21st Century Economy*, New York, St. Martin's Press, 2016.

18. Perlman, C., "From Product to Platform: John Deere Revolutionizes Farming," submitted to the Harvard Business School Digital Initiative at: https://digital.hbs.edu/platform-digit/submission/from-product-to-platform-john-deere-revolutionizes-farming/

19. Sundararajan, Arun, *The Sharing Economy: The End of Employment and the Rise of Crowd-Based Capitalism*, Cambridge, MIT Press, 2016.

20. BlaBlaCar, "In Trust We Trust," May 19, 2017, posted on Medium at https://medium.com/blablacar/inside-story-10-in-trust-we-trust-a8ca22359bc9.

21. Cusumano, Michael A., Gawer, Annabelle, and Yoffie, David B., *The Business of Platforms: Strategy in the Age of Digital Competition, Innovation, and Power*, New York, Harper Business, 2019.

22. Clauss, Thomas, et. al., "The perception of value of platform-based business models in the sharing economy: Determining the drivers of user loyalty," Review of Managerial Science, November 2018.

23. Schenker, Jennifer L., "The Platform Economy," January 19, 2019, posted on Medium at https://innovator.news/the-platform-economy-3c09439b56

24. Van Alstyne, Marshall W., Parker, Geoffrey G., and Choudary, Sangeet Paul, "Pipelines, Platforms, and the New Rules of Strategy," Harvard Business Review, April 2016.

25. Moazed, Alex, and Johnson, Nicholas L., *Modern Monopolies: What it Takes to Dominate the 21st Century Economy*, New York, St. Martin's Press, 2016.

About Anna Noakes Schulze

Anna Noakes Schulze is Senior Partner for Customer Experience at Ecodynamics, a platform economy and digital business consultancy. Previously, she founded SunflowerUX, a digital customer experience advisory and held senior user experience roles with digital agencies in London.

Anna is a keynote speaker, TEDx speaker and coach, and startup mentor. She is a certified Customer Experience Specialist (CXS) and a member of the Customer Experience Professionals Association (CXPA). She is actively engaged in the CX community as an awards judge for user experience, digital CX, digital strategy, and digital transformation for various customer experience events and programs including the International Customer Experience Awards.

For over 20 years, Anna has been dedicated to building better digital experiences. She retains a single-minded focus on helping businesses realise the potential of digital platforms to connect and create value through great customer and partner experiences.

Contacts And Links

LinkedIn: *@annanoakesschulze*

Medium: *@AnnaNoakesSchulze*

Instagram: *@sunflower_ux*

TEDx Talk: Living Abroad Teaches Us the Power of Connections:

https://youtu.be/CuEA6mQl4As

Catch All Editions of Customer Experience

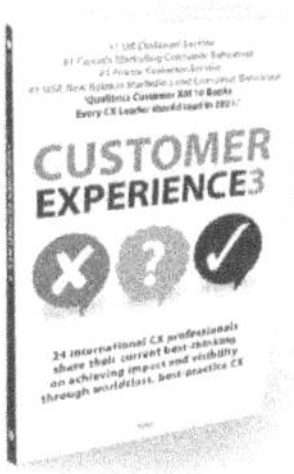

Customer Experience 1 (Kindle) *https://amzn.to/32JYM0j*

Customer Experience 1 (Book) *https://amzn.to/2LmB0BZ*

Customer Experience 2 (Kindle) *https://amzn.to/3928Oyx*

Customer Experience 2 (Book) *https://amzn.to/3r9IBpX*

Customer Experience 3 (Kindle) *https://amzn.to/*

Customer Experience 3 (Book) *https://amzn.to/*

Would You Like To Contribute To Future Editions of *Customer Experience?*

Customer experience as a professional is growing and evolving on a daily basis. There are many examples of innovative thinking and projects that have made a huge difference around the world.

The idea of this book is to allow CX practitioners around the world to share their best-practice stories for the mutual benefit of everyone.

Our first outing of *Customer Experience* has been a #1 international best-ranked, bestseller in the categories of *Customer Service, Customer Relations, Customer Experience Management, Consumer Behaviour* and *Marketing and Sales.* Clearly, professionals want to stay right up-to-date with what's happening in *Customer Experience Management (CXM).*

We are actively looking for new contributors for our next edition of *Customer Experience.* If you would like to get involved in the next release, then get in touch. All you need a good story to share that you know will add value to the readership.

If you would like the *Writer's Guide,* please email Naeem Arif:

Naeem@NAConsulting.co.uk

Lightning Source UK Ltd.
Milton Keynes UK
UKHW020005270421
382663UK00005B/107